D0210815

SASHA

SASHA

The Life of
Alexandra Tolstoy

Catherine Edwards Sadler

G. P. Putnam's Sons
New York

Author's Note

All conversations herein have been taken from books and memoirs written by Alexandra Tolstoy and her relatives with permission of the Alexandra Tolstoy estate and the Tolstoy Foundation.

Copyright © 1982 by Catherine Edwards Sadler
All rights reserved. Published simultaneously in
Canada by General Publishing Co. Limited, Toronto.
Printed in the United States of America
First impression.
Book design by Nanette Stevenson
Library of Congress Cataloging in Publication Data
Sadler, Catherine Edwards.
Sasha, the life of Alexandra Tolstoy.
Bibliography: p.
Includes index.
1. Tolstoy, Alexandra, 1884–1979.
2. Tolstoy, Leo, graf, 1828–1910—Biography.
3. Daughters—Soviet Union—Biography.
4. Novelists, Russian—19th century—Biography.
5. Tolstoy, Leo, graf, 1828–1910—Philosophy. I. Title.
PG3385.S2   891.73′3   [B]   81-17911   AACR2
ISBN 0-399-20857-7

Front jacket photo: the tea table in the park in 1892.
(from left: Misha, Tolstoy, Vanichka, Lev, Sasha, Andrei,
Tanya, Sonya and Masha.)
Back jacket photo and frontispiece: Sasha and her father in 1908.
All photographs are courtesy of the Tolstoy Foundation.

To Alan

ACKNOWLEDGMENTS

The author would like to thank the Tolstoy Foundation for their support and assistance throughout the writing of this book and for the use of their extensive Tolstoy library.

A debt of gratitude is owed to Professor Carole Emerson for her stimulating teaching of Russian literature and history and her invitation to me to travel with her to the Soviet Union. I could not have wished for a more informed companion while visiting both the Tolstoy home in Moscow and the Tolstoy family estate of Yasnaya Polyana.

A special note of thanks goes to Professor Catherine Wolkonsky, Alexandra Tolstoy's close friend, secretary and literary assistant, who gave me access to unpublished memoirs and family photographs. She also answered many questions and read over the entire manuscript, much to its betterment.

And lastly, I must thank Alexandra Tolstoy herself, whose assistance and cooperation were invaluable. I am deeply saddened that she did not live to see this book complete.

THE TOLSTOY FAMILY

LEV (LEO) NIKOLAYEVICH TOLSTOY
(*1828–1910*)
SOFYA (SONYA) ANDREYEVNA TOLSTOY
(*1844–1919*)

their children:
SERGEI LVOVICH (*1863–1947*)
TATYANA (TANYA) LVOVNA (*1864–1950*)
ILYA LVOVICH (*1866–1933*)
LEV LVOVICH (*1869–1945*)
MARYA (MASHA) LVOVNA (*1870–1906*)
PYOTR LVOVICH (*1872–1873*)
NIKOLAI LVOVICH (*1874–1875*)
VARVARA LVOVNA (*1875–1875*)
ANDREI LVOVICH (*1877–1916*)
MIKHAIL (MISHA) LVOVICH (*1879–1944*)
ALEKSEI LVOVICH (*1881–1886*)
ALEXANDRA (SASHA) LVOVNA (*1884–1979*)
IVAN (VANICHKA) LVOVICH (*1888–1895*)

THE USE OF NAMES

There are three kinds of names used in Russia. These are the given, or Christian name; the patronymic, or middle name; and the family, or last name. The patronymic is derived from the father's given name and usually ends in "evich" or "ovich" for males and "evna" or "ovna" for females. When addressing a person it is usual for both the given and the patronymic to be used.

Given	Patronymic	Family
LEV	NIKOLAYEVICH	TOLSTOY
ALEXANDRA	LVOVNA	TOLSTOY
MIKHAIL	LVOVICH	TOLSTOY
SOFYA	ANDREYEVNA	TOLSTOY

Lev Tolstoy's father's given name was Nikolai, hence Lev was given the patronymic Nikolayevich. The patronymic for Lev is Lvovna in the female and Lvovich in the male, therefore Lev's children all had one or the other as their middle name. Sofya's father's given name was Andrei, hence her patronymic was Andreyevna.

The given and the patronymic names are used out of respect. Only in speaking with a close friend or relative is the patronymic dropped and the diminutive, or nickname, used instead: Sasha for Alexandra, Misha for Mikhail, Masha for Maria, Sonya for Sofya, and so on.

PROLOGUE

There are few names in world literature as respected and renowned as that of Count Leo Tolstoy. He is considered one of the world's greatest writers and is famed for his capacity to capture people's innermost thoughts and his ability to create the complex portrait of nineteenth-century Russian life he projected in his works.

Lev Nikolayevich Tolstoy was born in 1828 at Yasnaya Polyana, his family estate 120 miles south of Moscow. He and his brothers were orphaned as children, and were brought up by aunts and educated by tutors. From his earliest youth Tolstoy wrote his experiences and reflections in diaries, a practice he was to maintain thoughout his long life. At sixteen he left home to study languages and law at the University of Kazan, only to leave in 1849 without receiving his degree, upon inheriting Yasnaya Polyana. He considered it his duty to devote himself to the running of the estate and the care of his peasants. Upon his return, he tried to educate the peasants. However, they were suspicious of their master's unusual behavior and his efforts soon came to nothing. Tolstoy then spent a number of years in Moscow and the army, after which he wrote a trilogy of books entitled *Childhood, Boyhood,* and *Youth,* based on his early diaries. In 1862 he finally settled at Yasnaya Polyana with his wife, Sofya Andreyevna Behrs. They began to raise their large family and he wrote the novels for which he is most famous: *War and Peace*—a lengthy epic on Napoleon's invasion of Russia in 1812—and *Anna Karenina*—a romantic novel of tragic love.

By 1876 Leo Tolstoy, as he was and is known by the English-speaking world, had begun to develop a religious philosophy based on Christian love, nonviolence, and simplifying life to its most basic, pure form. He dedicated his remaining years and his later works to these religious beliefs. His desire to give up family life and all worldly goods created a drama in his home equal to any of his early novels. Only his daughter Alexandra, or Sasha, as she was called, stood behind him in his final efforts to break away from worldly commitments. After Tolstoy's death in 1910 it was Sasha who dedicated herself to his beliefs and memory, striving to attain her father's high level of dedication and achievement. This is her story.

PART ONE

Lev Nikolayevich

1

SASHA STOOD AT THE TOP OF THE HILL, SILHOU-
etted against the clear Russian sky, her brown shoul-
der-length hair blowing in the summer wind. She was
not a pretty child, her shoulders were too wide and
her face too broad. But she had those unmistakable
Tolstoy gray eyes, and her determined look mirrored
her father's. He stood beside her now, his large hand
holding hers. His long wiry beard was streaked with
white and his face was deeply wrinkled, making him
look older than his sixty-two years, and more like an
old man than the father of a six-year-old girl.

Together they gazed out over Yasnaya Polyana,
the Tolstoy family estate. From the hilltop, they
could see down to the large white house with its
garden and sweeping front lawn and the long row of
linden trees leading to its entrance. Beyond was the
birch grove and the Zasseka wood and the winding
Voronka River where Tolstoys had swum for over a
hundred years. Along its banks sprawled the village

of Yasnaya Polyana, whose peasants had once been owned by the Tolstoys.

At the foot of the hill, the meadow was freshly cut. The discarded coats of the mowers lay to one side, cast off as the day grew warm. More than forty men mowed in a snakelike row. Behind them the women tossed and stacked the hay. Sasha could see her sister Masha among them. She was dressed like the other women and girls in a colorful smock with a bright red kerchief tied tightly over her thickly plaited blond hair. Sasha was not surprised to see her there. Slim, shy Masha was not like other twenty-one-year-old girls whose fathers were wealthy men. She did not care for fancy-dress balls or idle gossip like their other sister, Tanya. Masha was quite extraordinary, in fact. She spent her days helping others and was known and loved by the peasants throughout the region. There were many, including their own mother, who did not understand or approve of Masha's spending her time in this way. But Sasha looked up to her sister and envied her closeness to their father.

Lev Nikolayevich let go her hand and knelt down to the yellowing blades of grass. Sasha knew well what was troubling her father. It was time for harvest, but the hay was not as high and the yield would not be as good as in previous years. In recent days talk in the village was almost always about the possibility of famine. It had not rained in some time and rumors of crop failure were coming up from the south.

The villagers prayed to the saints portrayed in their religious paintings, called icons. They prayed that famine would not come to Tula, the province in which Yasnaya Polyana was situated, because then there would not be enough food to keep them through the inevitable harsh winter, let alone any extra for the small profit they depended on to buy clothes and other necessities. Sasha had turned away on hearing this talk for she did not like to think about anything that could upset her father.

Sasha treasured moments alone with him above all else. She was much too young to read Lev Nikolayevich Tolstoy's books, but she knew that he was a famous writer, well known not only in Russia but throughout the world. Her English governess, who called him "Leo" Tolstoy, often said that he was one of the greatest writers of the nineteenth century and had captured the essence of Russian life in his books *War and Peace* and *Anna Karenina*. Certainly, people were always coming to Yasnaya Polyana and to their winter home in Moscow to seek his advice and interview him. There were always mounds of letters to answer and constant requests for articles or comments on current events. All of this left little time for normal family life, or Sasha. And so Sasha treasured moments alone with her father such as this.

Lev Tolstoy straightened his tall, lean body and started down the hill toward the mowers. Sasha watched as he quickened his step to join the sea of red and black. As he approached, the mowers stopped their work. One of the men handed him a newly sharpened scythe. He took it and stepped into line. Soon he too was caught in the spell of harvesting, his white peasant blouse open to the waist, his tanned hands holding the heavy tool as though he had been born to such work.

Sasha lifted her skirts and raced down to the meadow. Today she would work beside her sister and father.

There was a time, not so long ago, when Lev Nikolayevich Tolstoy did not toil beneath a summer sun . . . a time when he played with his many children and taught them himself. He had been born in 1828 into the wealthiest, most affluent class of Russia. It was expected that he, as a landowner of noble birth, would live a life of luxury befitting his rank—occupying himself with such pastimes as hunting, fishing, and the running of his estate. When he married Sofya Andreyevna Behrs in 1862 and moved to Yasnaya Polyana she expected and wanted their children to be taken care of by nurses and governesses, the boys to be educated first by foreign tutors and then at universities, the girls to go out into society to meet husbands of their own class. This was the way it had been in Russia for as long as anyone could remember and there seemed no reason to change. But Lev Nikolayevich did change. He began to question the entire way of life in Russia from the rigid class structure to the authority of the Russian Orthodox Church. More and more he tried to live according to Christ's example—simplifying his life, working with the peasants, not drinking alcohol or smoking or eating meat. He began to question his right to own land or possessions when others had no opportunities for such advantages. He spoke of giving his land to the peasants and rejecting the profits from his books. He stopped writing the novels which had increased his wealth and fame. Instead he wrote religious pamphlets and reading primers to teach the peasants who he believed were naturally close to God. It was not long before he had a great following of people who wanted to dedicate themselves to his "Tolstoyan" way of life. More and more the house was filled with visitors and followers come to pay homage to their new spiritual leader.

Lev Nikolayevich would have liked his wife, Sonya, as she was called, to join him in his "rebirth." But she could not give up either her religious beliefs or the way of life she felt was best for her children. And so Sasha's parents often fought over how to bring up their children and over the constant presence of strangers whom Sonya called "the dark ones" because she felt they brought gloom into her home.

Sasha could not remember the last time she had sat down to a meal for fewer than twenty at their long table in the dining room. It was true that the family was large—six boys and three girls—but the older ones were often not at home and the youngest, Vanichka, ate in the nursery. When Masha was Sasha's age supper had been a time when her father could relax and joke, when the children would hide under the table from their mother or ride about the carpet which their father pulled all over the room.

The Tolstoyans had changed all that. They did not approve of such gaiety. To them it seemed that one ought to think of God all the time. Sasha, whose proper name was Alexandra Lvovna, had been born in 1884 after his "rebirth." She had not known her father when he was more carefree, but each of her older sisters and brothers had fond memories of that happy period. Sometimes she could not help but be jealous of them and of the Tolstoyans who commanded so much of his attention. Nor could she help longing for a time when he would pay attention to her as he did the older ones.

Sasha's days were filled with studies and activities and each summer her cousins, the Kuzminskys, came to visit. Often they would all go out fruit and vegetable picking for her mother's preserving and canning. Sometimes they played croquet on the front lawn or went to swim in the river. At night someone would play the guitar or piano and they would join in singing. But Sasha knew how her father disapproved of such frivolity. She had often heard him argue with her mother about the parties and comforts at Yasnaya Polyana and their house in Moscow. Knowing this, it was hard for Sasha to enjoy herself. Whenever she became too caught up in the fun, she would scold herself for not being serious and useful. She even tried to pattern herself, like Masha, on her father's teachings. She refused to eat meat and defiantly took the ribbons from her hair and the shoes from her feet. But her efforts to be "Tolstoyan" came to no good, for her mother thought she was willful and her father did not notice at all.

Sasha's adoration of her father was not unusual. There was something about his soft-spoken voice and his penetrating eyes that attracted people to him. He had a godlike quality which his glowing white beard and bushy brows enhanced. Sasha never thought to be angry or hurt when he seemed to ignore her, for she knew that he was a busy and important man. When he was away from home she would often go to his study where the familiar smell of leather mingling with old paper always reminded her of him. And there were books—thousands and thousands of books. Sasha liked to decipher her father's name, which so often appeared on their covers. Alone in his study, Sasha would imagine him sitting at his great desk, poring over books on religion and history, furiously making notes in his near-illegible scrawl. Other times she'd see him sitting in his battered old armchair, a painter or sculptor busily trying to capture the great man's likeness. Sometimes she'd even imagine herself as a grown-up working right at his side. That was her secret dream. In the meantime she contented herself with having him close by.

But even this was not to be. A letter from the south brought news that everyone's fears of a famine were true. Tolstoy was needed to help the suffering peasants. One Sunday evening he gathered his family together and told them that he would soon be leaving for Ryazan in the south. He was taking the older girls, Masha and Tanya, to help him, and Sonya was to take the younger children to Moscow for the winter. Within a week Sasha, her brothers Misha and Andrei and little Vanichka, along with an entire entourage of servants—from footmen to seamstresses—were aboard a train bound for Moscow. Sasha did not know when she would see her father again or what lay in store for him. Nor could she know then that their day in the fields would be the last they would share together for a good many years to come.

2

THE TOLSTOY HOUSE IN KHAMOVNIKI STREET WAS not in a fashionable part of Moscow, but it had a quaint charm about it, and the entire family always enjoyed spending winters there. Sasha's father had bought the house in 1881, when his older sons, Sergei, Ilya and Lev, were of high school and university age and their educations could no longer be limited to private teachers. Their mother, Sonya, had been overjoyed at the purchase for she had been born and raised in Moscow and loved the teas and balls for which it was famous. In past winters Sasha and her brothers Andrei and Misha had made a miniature skating rink on a small flat area behind the house. Back and forth they'd carry the buckets of water, day after day, until great sheets of ice formed. Then Sasha and the others would twist and turn and glide happily across the ice. But this winter even the thought of that wonderful rink did not interest her and the cozy house with its mazelike paths perfect for hide-and-seek held few charms. She wandered aimlessly through the house's halls and richly decorated rooms—every keepsake, each small object, reminding her that her father and sisters were gone.

Of all the children it was Sasha who suffered the most from her father's and sisters' absence. The older boys were away and the younger ones, Misha and Andrei, had each other for company and could not be bothered with their younger sister. That left only little Vanichka, whom Sasha loved. But he was their mother's pet and often left Sasha out of their games. Sasha could never forget one time when she thought everyone in the house had gone out, leaving her alone. She had run frantically from room to room searching for someone—anyone. At last she had come upon her mother with Vanichka sitting on her lap. He was telling her a story he had made up, while she wrote it down upon a piece of paper. Sasha's face was wet from crying, but her mother was too involved with her beautiful little son to notice. How Sasha had hated her mother then—for her love of Vanichka, for her arguments with Father. Sonya did not see how much Sasha needed and wanted her mother's love and approval. From that moment on it was to Masha and Tanya that Sasha turned for comfort and love.

Masha was particularly sensitive to Sasha's hurt and loneliness. She often sat Sasha down on her hard bed and cheered her with stories of the Yasnaya Polyana peasants. When Sasha found a maimed bird in the park, it was to Masha that she went with it; when she scraped a knee trying to climb the garden trellis, it was Masha whom she let dress the wound.

11

Tanya also found time for Sasha. She was often busy with her friends and engagements but whenever she spied a sulking Sasha she would grab her arm and drag her into the garden where she'd set out her paints and sketch pad. Then the two sisters, twenty years apart in age, would paint together side by side.

In Tanya and Masha, Sasha felt that she had people who understood her and thought she was special. But this winter, with her father and her two sisters away, Sasha felt alone with no one to turn to.

She spent most of her days looking out the window at her father's old horse, Malchik, as he grazed on the grass or chased their Eskimo dog, Belka, into the park. A new tutor gave her plenty of work, but Sasha could not keep her mind on it. All she could think of were her father and two sisters. She envisioned them stranded in some remote spot, wandering about the countryside in freezing, brutal blizzards.

Sasha's imaginings were actually not far from the truth. Letters arrived from her father and sisters describing the abominable conditions in the south. They told of peasants wandering the streets in rags and of children begging pitifully for food. On arriving in Ryazan Lev Nikolayevich and his two daughters had been shocked at the conditions they found. The misery was extreme. The peasants, who relied entirely on the crops for their livelihood, were starving and freezing. They had no money to buy wood. Their two-room huts, called izbas, had become igloos. To keep the huge pechs, or stoves, lit they had ripped the thatching from their roofs to burn.

12

Sasha's mother, Sofya Andreyevna, was as distressed over the situation as Sasha. She worried constantly about her husband and daughters. She wanted desperately to help in the famine relief. Stuck in Moscow, she too felt cut off and useless. Her husband had written letters to the Tsar asking for aid. But the Tsar had not responded. Money was needed to buy food and to set up kitchens where the peasants could come to eat for free. Sonya decided to appeal to her fellow aristocrats for help. She wrote a heartfelt letter and sent it to all the national newspapers. It was published and became an immediate sensation. People began to arrive at the house with bundles filled with dry goods, clothes, and medicines. Letters and packages came in each post, everyone volunteering money or merchandise to help the famine victims. The house in Khamovniki Street teemed with activity.

Sasha hadn't realized that her mother felt so strongly about the peasants' situation. For the first time she saw her mother committed to something other than the house, her husband, or Vanichka. Sasha too wanted to help, so she ran errands, sorted letters, carried messages and she loved every minute. Her father might not know what she was doing, but Sasha felt that she was helping him in his great work.

In Ryazan, Tolstoy wrote letters to newspapers around the world describing the terrible conditions and asking for help. His pleas were heard. In the United States Minnesota millers sent free flour and Kansas farmers loaded bushel after bushel of corn into crates stamped RUSSIA. People everywhere were shocked at the Russian government's seeming lack of concern. The Tsar and his ministers soon found themselves in an uncomfortable position and they blamed Tolstoy for stirring up world opinion with his highly emotional letters. Many Tsarists began to see Tolstoy as a threat to the stability of the government. In their view he was far too popular with the discontented peasants and could lead them to revolution. So they tried to shake the people's love for him. They spread rumors that he was a heretic— an Antichrist—sure that this would set the people against him since the vast majority of peasants were devout Russian Orthodox Catholics. They banned his books, they said he planned to assassinate the Tsar. Tolstoy heard the rumors and stories but they did not bother him. Obviously the Tsar's men had not studied his pamphlets, which clearly stated his beliefs, or they would have known that he believed in God and Christ, was dedicated to helping the people and abhorred violence of any kind. The only revolution he was interested in was a spiritual one.

In one year he set up 246 kitchens in four districts that fed thirteen thousand people daily. One hundred and twenty-four kitchens for children were started where special nutritional foods were served; three thousand children were fed daily. With the money Sasha's mother sent to her husband, food and medical supplies were bought. Seed was given out so that new crops could be planted. Schools were established in the second year so that young and old could better their situations in the future once the famine ended. Sasha hoped and prayed for the survival of the new crop. But it did not survive. Worse still, an epidemic of typhoid followed the crop failure. Sonya, fearing for her family's lives, issued direct orders that Lev, Masha, and Tanya come home at last.

Sasha eagerly awaited their arrival. In the two years since the start of the famine they had returned to Moscow a number of times, but now they were coming home to stay. In those two years her mother and Vanichka had grown even closer and Sasha longed for the return of her two allies and the father she idolized. She had dreamed of returning to Yasnaya Polyana and resuming life as it was before their departure—perhaps improving on it now that she was older and could do more to help them. But once home, all three seemed changed. Her sisters were so serious now, like the Tolstoyans at Yasnaya Polyana. They had seen great hardships in the south and it had caused them to think about their beliefs and futures. Both were firmly dedicated to assisting their father with his work. They no longer seemed interested in what Sasha did or thought. Her father was sullen and moody and the luxuries in the house bothered him more than ever. He seemed distant, aloof, and spent most of his time with his followers, who had flocked immediately to their leader upon his return.

The famine had secured Tolstoy's position as a hero of the people. In the eyes of millions of Russians he was like a father, fighting for his children and their rights. But for his own child he had no time or interest. To him his daughter Alexandra Lvovna was a mere child, unable to think or feel independently. He saw luxuries around her and assumed that she would grow up to value those material things more than the spiritual ones he was constantly striving for in his work and personal life. It was going to be up to Sasha to find a way of making him see that she deserved his recognition.

3

Sasha may have wished that life would return to the way it had once been, but instead it grew more difficult with each day. At Yasnaya Polyana her father plunged into his work and seemed finally to lose all interest in family life. His relations with his wife grew increasingly strained and they often argued. The mood of the entire house was tense and there seemed little anyone could do to ease the tension.

Sasha's mother fretted constantly over her husband's distance and their daily arguments. They were always about the same thing: his desire to give away his properties and monies to the peasants and the constant presence of the "dark ones" in the house. She was sure that they were infecting her husband with their seriousness and forcing him to renounce those ties to the material world that still bound him.

Brought up in an elegant Moscow house, Sofya Andreyevna Behrs had expected her married life to be filled with the occupations typical of an aristocratic couple: balls, parties, trips, and the mutual enjoyment of bringing up a family. Her husband was a count with a country estate and numerous servants and peasants at the time of their marriage. For years they had shared such a life and were happy, or so she had thought. He had written his novels and she had worked at being a good mother and wife. They had both tried to give their children a sound religious upbringing. But when Lev Nikolayevich had begun to abandon his old beliefs and habits, she could not join him in his new philosophies and life-style. How could she throw away the security and future of her children by giving away their income and land? What would become of them without proper education? How would they manage without money? The older boys were constantly asking her for help. And her daughters? What would they do without inheritances? Should they become seamstresses and nurses?

Had her life been different, Sofya Andreyevna might have been willing to join her husband in his "rebirth." But with nine children to care for she could not. So she fought and she argued, watching over the house and the property like a hawk, jealously protecting the things she felt provided her family with safety and security. What wounded her gravely was that her husband and children judged her for her selfishness and materialism. They did not understand that she was clinging to the things that gave meaning to her life. It seemed to her that only her youngest child, Vanichka, understood and had sympathy for her. Now more than ever she spent her days with him.

Vanichka was the most beautiful of the Tolstoy children. He had large inquisitive blue eyes and golden ringlets that framed his pale, delicate face. He possessed the remarkable ability of being able to sense other people's feelings and thoughts. Unlike Sasha, who kept her feelings bottled up inside and never seemed able to speak with her father, Vanichka would brazenly walk up to him and tell him precisely what he thought. When Vanichka laughed a room was suddenly filled with brightness. He was always thinking of others and when someone acted meanly it hurt him deeply.

But it was not only Vanichka's and her mother's closeness which upset Sasha. Her father had openly shunned her on two specific occasions. In the winter of 1894, when Sasha was ten, a series of children's balls were given by friends of her mother's. Sasha had not wanted to go because she felt awkward at social gatherings and she knew that her father disliked this type of amusement. But her mother insisted and at last Sasha had agreed to go. Sonya hired a fashionable hairdresser to do up Sasha's hair in the latest court fashion. He piled her hair high on her head, filling it with powder and pins. When she gazed into the hallway mirror, she was horrified. What if her father were to see her like this?

She ran from the house into the waiting carriage. At the ball she began to forget her anxiety and enjoy the music and the young people. She even agreed to dance with a shy young boy. But during the dance she heard tapping· at the windowpane nearest her. She looked over and saw her father and Masha peering through. Sasha broke away from her partner. She wanted to run outside and explain everything to her father. But when she turned back, they were gone.

Another time, she had just sat down at a party, feeling a bit dizzy from the iced champagne, when suddenly she saw her father's dog, Belka, pushing his way through the crowd followed by her father. Sasha took a deep breath. But just as she was about to speak, a group of adults recognized and surrounded him and Sasha missed the opportunity to defend herself.

Everything Sasha did seemed to go wrong. When she tried to please her mother, her father's worst fears about her seemed confirmed. When she tried to please her father, her mother considered her troublesome. Only seven-year-old Vanichka sensed his sister's growing confusion and in his own way he tried to help. He was always trying to include her in his games and was upset when he was given something and Sasha was not. Often he would look up at the person and say hopefully, "And Sasha? What about Sasha?" Sasha recognized her little brother's efforts and loved him all the more.

Vanichka was a frail child and it was not uncommon for him to run a high fever. In the winter of 1895 he fell ill with fever as he had so many times before. After three days he started to recover and the entire household relaxed. But the fever struck again and his temperature remained at an alarming 104 degrees. "It isn't anything, mama," he told Sonya.

"Don't worry, Sasha. Everything will turn out well," he assured his worried sister. "Don't cry; why are you crying?" he scolded his nurse.

Doctors were called in. They diagnosed scarlet fever. Within days dark circles developed around his eyes and a blue vein started to show up across his pale face. On the fourth day Sasha heard a wild cry coming from the nursery. The voice was so terrible that it took a moment for her to recognize it as her mother's. Sasha tried to go to the nursery, but the nurse held her back and insisted she return to her own room.

When it was late and no one was about, Sasha slipped into the nursery. The dark room smelled of hyacinths and incense. A chanter sat in the corner of the room reading the psalter under her breath. On the table in the center of the room was a small wooden coffin with candles all around it. The wax was low and dripped onto the cloth.

Sasha tiptoed over to the coffin. It was open, in the Russian manner. Slowly she raised herself and peered in. It was Vanichka sleeping there, so different and yet so peaceful. She bent toward him and kissed his small forehead. It was cold and waxlike. "This is not Vanichka," she wanted to scream. "This is not my brother!" For a moment she stood looking into the coffin, oblivious of the room, the chanter, even Vanichka. Then she saw his face clearly and knew that he was dead. She ran from the room sobbing.

In the days that followed, gloom hung over the house. Masha walked lightly from room to room, caring for her grief-stricken mother, her silent father, the shaken old nurse. She made sure Misha and Andrei stayed out of mischief and went to Sasha and tried to comfort her as she had before she had gone away to help during the famine. At first Sonya wandered about the house like a mad woman, clutching Vanichka's toys to her, crying, "Why is God so unjust to me? Why did he take Vanichka?" and finally, in a moment of hysteria she cried out, "Why Vanichka? Why not Sasha?" She did not know that Sasha stood in the doorway. Nor could she have foreseen the effect those words would have in the years ahead.

Both Sonya and Sasha suffered terribly at Vanichka's death. Sasha had lost the only ally she had amid what she thought were enemies. In the days following the funeral, she often tried to remember how he had looked and acted. But she could not. Only the image of him lying in his coffin took shape. The scent of hyacinths and incense pursued her ruthlessly. Had her mother been able to turn toward Sasha they would have realized that both were going through similar emotions and their lives might have turned out quite differently. But Sonya's words burned in Sasha's heart and were to become a barrier neither could ever truly cross.

Lev Nikolayevich spent much of his day trying to understand why God had taken his youngest son— the one child he had hoped would someday be his spiritual heir. He tried to accept Vanichka's death as an act of God, and often felt that Vanichka had been too good for this world. "What does it mean that he is dead?" he would say. "There is no death. He is not dead because we still love him and so he continues to live in us." Aware of his wife's despair, Lev Nikolayevich tried to be tender to her. Since she could not bear to be alone, he, Tanya, and Masha took turns staying with her day and night. She went to church often where she continually prayed for her dead son. Her husband, who would no longer set foot inside a church since he did not agree with the way in which the church presented Christ's teachings, waited outside until she was ready to go home. He tried to take her mind off her grief by awakening a sense of concern for others and so took her to visit prisons and purchase books for the inmates. But nothing interested her and everyone feared that she would wander about the house dressed from head to foot in black mourning for a long time to come.

But then quite suddenly Sonya found something that lifted her spirits—music. She pored over scores, practiced every day, went to concerts. This new interest helped her feel happy again and she began to speak about the new Tsar's coronation in the spring. She talked of taking Misha and Sasha to see one of the most beautiful of all Russian ceremonies. And although Lev Nikolayevich Tolstoy cared little for such extravagance and pomp, he urged his wife to go.

4

RATHER THAN OPEN THE HOUSE IN MOSCOW FOR the coronation, Sonya agreed to stay at the home of a friend. The house was situated directly on the main avenue leading to the Kremlin, an ancient walled fortress within Moscow where the Tsars of Russia had once lived. From the house's balcony they could watch the festivities as if in a private box at the theater.

The royal entry into the city on May 25, 1896, was the first event, and Sasha and Misha watched breathlessly as the Imperial Guard and Cossacks marched past. They were dressed in their formal uniforms adorned with gold braiding and ornaments. The parade seemed endless . . . there were hundreds of horse-drawn carriages carrying the nobility and court staff. Finally the new Tsar, Nicholas II, rode by. He was young and handsome, his hand fixed in a constant salute. He wore a dark army tunic and rode a huge white horse. Behind him a golden carriage with the imperial crown on its beam was drawn by six white horses exactly like his own. Inside the carriage sat the future Tsarina, his new wife, Alix of Hesse-Darmstadt, or Alexandra, as she would be called. Sasha had never seen such opulence and show, not even at the parties and balls she had attended. Despite her efforts not to be interested in the goings-on—wanting to be "Tolstoyan" and knowing what her father thought of such fanfare and wasted money—she could not help herself. This was history in the making, the start of a new reign, and she was witness to it.

Even more exciting than the royal entry into the city were the processions of the following day—coronation day. Now it was the people who marched, thousands and thousands of people. There were balalaika bands and gypsy bands and cartloads of peasants from every region of Russia, from Sasha's Tula to far-off Uzbek. The peasants were dressed in colorful headdresses and blouses. Many wore glittering jewelry about their necks and arms. They sang native songs as their carts rumbled along the avenue and often jumped out of their carts to dance.

Many of these peasants had come to Moscow for an open-air feast at Khodynka Meadow. The feast was being given by the imperial government with free beer and food for all. It was said that the new Tsar and Tsarina would appear. But that was tomorrow. There was still much celebrating to do today. The city seemed to scream from the excitement of it all . . . the church bells and the rumble of carts and the clipclop of horses and the sound of voices raised in song and laughter. There was nothing to do but join in!

Lev Nikolayevich, of course, would have disagreed. He felt that making such a fuss over the Tsar's ascension to total and frighteningly absolute rule was pure folly. To him a coronation represented the oppression of the people. It was the continuation of an archaic system which had not adapted itself to modern times. Nonetheless, he couldn't help but join his fellow liberal Russians in hoping that the young Tsar would bring about some sorely needed reforms—perhaps the constitution his grandfather had been on the verge of signing at his untimely death.

It was the new Tsar's grandfather, Alexander II, who had been responsible for the Emancipation Act of 1861 which supposedly freed the peasants. Before that time the majority of peasants were owned by rich nobles and were known as serfs. There were two types of serfs—domestic slaves who worked in the house as coachmen, grooms, cooks and so on, and serfs who worked in the fields. The peasants rented communal land which they could work for profit and food. They paid the rent for this land through labor and taxes, usually paid in a combination of money, cloth, and livestock. Usually each labor unit of one man, one woman and one horse owed three days of labor to the landlord each week. Often a family of two labor units would send one member to work for the landlord six days a week while another worked the communal land for the household and the rent. The serf had no civil rights, no say in government, no constitutional protection, and no opportunities for education or social betterment. The Russian peasant was ignorant and poor, living to meet the landlord's demands, fearing harsh weather and famine which could destroy his livelihood. However, most peasants were highly religious and accepted their lot as the will of God. The Emancipation Act of 1861 abolished serfdom in that the peasants could no longer be owned and it gave them the right to buy land with government-loaned money. But it did not free them since they still had to work the land while paying someone for the right to do so.

A constitution would have spelled out their rights for the first time. But on the eve of its approval, Alexander II was killed by a terrorist bomb. The terrorists were part of an ever-growing revolutionary movement in Russia. They were not satisfied with emancipations and constitutions. They wanted the destruction of serfdom and the Tsar's absolute, or autocratic, rule.

Alexander II's son, Alexander III, came to power hating the liberal revolutionaries who had killed his father. Thus began thirteen years of harsh rule in which all opposition to the Tsar was met with banishment or imprisonment. However, despite his lack of understanding or sympathy for his people, Alexander did realize the importance of developing industry and building up the economy. And he understood that industry could only be developed by linking the hundreds of isolated villages across Russia. To start, he made an alliance with France, Russia's first western ally. Through this alliance, Alexander obtained loans which enabled him to start a huge railway network. In this he contributed greatly to his country's progress, for the railway enabled Russia's industry to prosper, communications systems to develop and provided people with greater mobility. It was unfortunate that he was not as far-thinking in his social policies as he was in his economic ones. His abrupt death in 1895 shocked everyone. But gradually that shock subsided and hope—hope that his son, Nicholas II, would create freedoms for his people—sprung up in its place.

But at the age of twenty-six, Nicholas II was ill-prepared to become Tsar. He leaned heavily on his ministers for advice. Three months after his father's death, he announced that he would follow his father's policy of total autocracy. There would be neither reforms nor a constitution. Still, the peasants continued to be loyal. To them he was the Batiushka-Tsar, the father of the people. He was closer to God than to man. While they might curse the tax collectors and the petty officials, to them the Tsar could do no wrong. They clung to the belief that he was unaware of their desires. If he knew, he would surely change the way things were.

So the people came to his coronation cheerfully. It was a time of celebration, a holiday. Pardons would be granted, prisoners would be released, and the feast at Khodynka Meadow would be grand.

The coronation was to take place on May 26, in the Kremlin, where for centuries the Tsars of Russia had lived, ruled, and worshiped. Now the Tsar lived in Peter the Great's "western city" of St. Petersburg, but tradition dictated the coronation be held in the ancient Kremlin. The Tolstoys had the great honor of being invited into the onion-domed Ouspensky Cathedral. By the time they made their way across the crowded square and were settled in the back of the huge, magnificent cathedral, the royal procession down the Red Staircase had begun.

Nicholas, his red beard cut square and his long mustache waxed so that it curled, wore a blue Imperial Guard's uniform with a vivid red sash across his chest and stiff braiding at the neck and shoulders. He walked slowly, arm in arm with his German wife. Twelve pages carried the long train of her silver-white court dress behind. A gold canopy decorated with magnificent ostrich plumes fluttered above their heads. When they reached the entrance to the church they turned and bowed low to the crowd. Priests touched their foreheads with holy water. The future Tsar and Tsarina of Russia entered the church.

Sasha hardly knew where to look first. The cathedral seemed ablaze with light and color. Candles shone everywhere, creating shadows and shapes on the gold-encrusted icons and murals that hung on the cathedral's walls. Priests in velvet robes with glimmering jeweled scepters stood at the golden altar in front of stained-glass windows that cast color throughout the huge church. Near the altar were two wonderful thrones, the larger totally covered in diamonds and rare gems, the smaller made of ivory. Modal Russian chants filled the air, sung by a silver-and-blue-dressed choir stationed to one side.

For five hours the ancient religious coronation ceremony went on and Sasha sat as if in a trance. She had gone to church weekly her whole life but never before had she been so moved or seen such grandeur.

Finally the coronation was over and the new emperor and empress of Russia slowly walked down the red velvet aisle into the daylight. Magnificent crowns adorned their heads and their shoulders were draped with lush cloaks embroidered with the imperial double-headed eagle. As they climbed the stairs once again the waiting crowd cheered and the sound of cannon thundered in the distance. Throughout the city church bells rang. The young couple bowed to their subjects and were gone. The reign of Nicholas and Alexandra had begun.

That night Sasha and Misha peered out the salon windows, hoping to catch a glimpse of royalty as they arrived for the coronation banquet and ball. When it was time to go to sleep, Sasha lay in bed, straining to hear the music of the ball which filled the Kremlin. It was only through sheer exhaustion that she finally fell asleep.

While Sasha slept, thousands of peasants assembled at Khodynka Meadow. The meadow was actually an imperial army training ground and was covered with ditches and trenches used in training exercises. These ditches made the meadow dangerous, but it was the only public field large enough to accommodate the huge crowd expected to come.

As the dawn approached the crowds grew. By daybreak five hundred thousand people had crowded onto the field, many drunk from all-night carousing. Finally the barrels of free beer arrived and the crowd started to move forward slowly. A rumor began to circulate that there was not enough beer for all. The crowd started to push. Peasants began running forward. Someone fell into a ditch, then another and another, but the crowd pushed on. Children were separated from mothers, men fell screaming, and still the crowd surged forward. In moments the meadow became a battlefield of moaning and bleeding people. By afternoon the Moscow hospitals were filled with the wounded and dead.

News of the disaster spread through the city. By evening it was being talked about in outlying areas of Moscow. Within days the news was common knowledge throughout the region.

Nicholas and Alexandra were stunned by the tragedy. They wanted to go into retreat to mourn. Nicholas immediately tried to cancel a ball planned for that evening by the French ambassador, but his ministers were afraid of offending their valuable ally. They insisted Nicholas and his bride attend. Reluctantly the impressionable Tsar agreed.

The following day the couple went from hospital to hospital visiting the wounded. They insisted the dead be buried in individual coffins rather than all together in a mass coffin as was the custom in such disasters. They gave money of their own to the families of the deceased. But their genuine sorrow and generosity could not alter what had already happened.

Sonya sobbed desperately when she heard of the tragedy. Her emotional state quickly reversed and the intense loss and despair which she had carried since her son's death returned. Frantically, she threw belongings into valises and by nightfall Sasha, Misha, and Sonya had boarded a train and were bound for Yasnaya Polyana.

By the time they reached home the village was

abuzz with talk of the heartless new Tsar and his German wife who could attend a ball only hours after the death of so many subjects. Most Russians, being highly superstitious, saw the entire incident as a foreshadowing of terrible things to come.

5

As the months passed it became clear to the
Tolstoy family that Sonya's mental state was unstable
and that she was truly not well. Her music became an
obsession which excluded all family members. Her
relations with Lev Nikolayevich grew steadily worse. He
began to speak more and more of a desire to break
away from her, the house, and Yasnaya Polyana for he
felt that life at home prevented him from attaining
peace within himself. He yearned for a quiet place
where he could grow closer to his God. With Sasha's
parents constantly at odds, it was not long before the
Tolstoy children one by one left the nest.

Ilya was the first to leave, first to join the army and
then to marry. Then Lev married a young Swedish
girl and moved to her homeland. The eldest, Sergei,
soon left to marry and settle permanently in Moscow.
Andrei joined the army and later married as well.
Even Masha and Tanya, who Sasha assumed would
stay at their father's side, eventually left home—

Masha to marry a young handsome cousin named Nikolai Obelensky and Tanya to marry a widower with six children, the oldest of whom was sixteen, the same age as Sasha. Only Sasha and her brother Misha remained and Misha eventually struck out on his own to marry his childhood sweetheart.

Lev Nikolayevich accepted his sons' departures but he was crushed by Masha's and Tanya's marriages. He could not understand how they could give up their spiritual upbringing and work dedicated to helping others for lives of drudgery as wives and mothers. He had hoped they would carry on his work after his death, which he now believed was near. He felt deserted and without an heir. Often he would think, *If only Vanichka had lived.* But Vanichka had not lived, and his daughters had rejected their father for lives of their own. Only Sasha remained. But he had long ago dismissed her as a serious candidate. He did not know that she had dreamed of working at his side since she was six years old and that she had spent much of her growing years thinking about his beliefs and trying to apply them to her life. Nor could he foresee that Sasha was about to go through a "rebirth" of her own—one that would unite them for the first time.

It was the sixth week of Lent when these changes began. The church bells of Moscow rang out, the vesper service was just over. Sasha was walking home from the service she had attended at the small church near Khamovniki Street. She had grown into a tall, awkward girl with broad shoulders and a strong but plain face whose telltale cheeks turned red at the slightest nervousness. The service and the choir of blind girls who sang there had inspired her with a desire to help her fellow man in some way. A bent, beggarly old woman stood next to her in church and Sasha helped her to light the candles before the sacred images, to sit down, to walk down the steep steps. Her black cape seemed green from wear and slightly moldy and her head shook in a most distracting manner. As Sasha stood behind her, guiding her down the stairs, she noticed lice crawling in her yellowish-gray hair and on the collar of her cloak. Sasha at first recoiled but then smiled and thought to herself, *She is dirty and smells, but I love her and am helping her.* Sasha felt deeply touched at her own virtue. *Tomorrow is Friday,* she thought. *I shall go to confession and be cleansed of all my sins*

Sasha felt inspired as she left the church. So involved was she in her thoughts that she nearly bumped into her father, who was taking a walk, a cane in his hand, his soft gray hat on his head, and an unbuttoned overcoat revealing his white peasant smock beneath.

"Where are you coming from?" he asked Sasha.

"From church," she replied nervously. Her father's eyes seemed to penetrate deep within her.

"Why are you wearing such a bright red scarf?"

Sasha remained silent. She looked down at the kerchief that she had tied so gaily about her neck that morning. He asked her again. Sasha stood, staring at her father. She thought to herself, *Bright red—yes, very bright, not modest but a bad scarf.* She felt sad, as if she had caught herself doing something she did not like. *And am I good?* she asked herself. *No, I am bad. Sort of false and insincere.*

*Above: Sofya Andreyevna with the younger children in 1890
(from left: Misha, Andrei, Sasha and Vanichka).
Facing page, above: The tea table in the park in 1892 (from left:
Misha, Tolstoy, Vanichka, Lev, Sasha, Andrei, Tanya, Sonya
and Masha).
Facing page, below: Yasnaya Polyana in the 1890's.*

Facing page, above: Yasnaya Polyana in the 1890's.
Facing page, below: The main street of Yasnaya Polyana village.
Above: Summer in the village.

Facing page, above: The house on Khamovniki Street, Moscow.
Facing page, below: Moscow in the 1890's.
Above: A family gathering in 1904 (from left, standing: Ilya,
Lev, Sasha, Sergei; sitting: Misha, Tanya, Sonya, Tolstoy, Masha
and Andrei).

Sasha went home deep in thought. She now realized that her feelings of the morning had been shallow, caused by her wanting to be good, rather than actually being good. *Would you have given all that you possess to that unwashed old woman?* she questioned herself. *Do you really love her? No, never! But if not, what is the value of your sentimental attentions to her and your touched virtuous mood?* Something was happening to Sasha. She was examining her own feelings and questioning things she had always taken for granted.

The next day she went to church with her mother. After a short vesper service the priest called for all those wanting confession. Sasha and her mother stood waiting their turn behind all the others. The old woman stood in front of them. She was leaning on her cane, shifting her weight back and forth. To Sasha, her head seemed to tremble even more than before. The priest approached. The old woman reached out toward him, but he walked past without even noticing her. He bowed to Sofya Andreyevna and said, "Please come up, Countess." The old woman backed away. Sasha was stunned. *How could the priest snub the old woman?* she thought angrily. *Aren't her needs as important as Mother's? And he calls himself a servant of God.*

The following day Sasha went to Holy Communion. She was dressed in a white gown. She listened to the priest's words and tried to be elated by them as she had in the past. But now she picked them apart. When the collection plate was passed it seemed to her that the more money one donated the larger the amount of wine and sacred bread one received.

When her mother called Sasha to get ready for

vespers the Saturday before Palm Sunday, Sasha told her that she was not going. At first her mother did not understand.

"Don't you feel well?" she asked, raising her palm to Sasha's forehead.

Sasha pulled away. "No, I'm all right. But I am not going to church anymore."

"But why?" Sonya asked, obviously disturbed at what she thought was another whim.

"I don't want to. It is all false."

Sofya Andreyevna was too shocked to speak. Her two older daughters, impressed with their father's teachings, had broken with the church many years before. She had hoped Sasha at least would stay on the true path. Upset, she went to her husband's study and remained inside for some time. When she came out, her eyes were red from crying.

"Father wants to see you," she told her youngest daughter and walked away.

Sasha walked into his study. Her father was sitting in his old armchair, a book in his large hands.

"Well now, why are you causing such grief to your mother? She has had quite enough lately, as you know." He looked sternly into Sasha's gray eyes—so like his own. "Why don't you want to go to church?"

"I can't," Sasha said, the tears beginning to well up.

"Don't cry," he said softly. But Sasha could not stop.

"Before abandoning the old, a person must know for sure whether he has anything new with which to replace it. Have you?"

"I don't know," Sasha answered under her breath.

"Then why do you hurt your mother's feelings and refuse to go to church with her?"

"It's all lying and falseness there. I can't," Sasha said.

"So that's what it is. But don't cry, darling," Lev Nikolayevich said.

Sasha looked up at her father. He had called her darling. Choking back tears and stammering terribly, she told him about the blind choir and the old lice-ridden woman and her virtuous mood and the priest and her response to him. Suddenly she was telling him how she had always tried to please him and her mother and had never been able to . . . how she had tried to follow his teachings without understanding the thought behind them. But that now she was beginning to respond to things on her own. She believed in God and wanted to live a meaningful, spiritual life. But it would have to be outside the Russian Orthodox Church.

"Just the same," he said thoughtfully, "tomorrow go to church with your mother one last time." He looked at Sasha as though she were an adult. Then he bent over and kissed her forehead. His eyes shone cheerfully.

Lev Nikolayevich had good reason to be suddenly cheerful. He had just discovered that his one remaining daughter was not the frivolous, nonquestioning girl he had taken her for. She possessed the inner spirit he admired most in a person. And she had come to his way of viewing the church and spiritualism on her own. He had found the spiritual heir he had always hoped for. She had been growing up in his midst all the time.

6

Since the beginning of nicholas ii's reign the people of Russia had been discontented because the reforms they had hoped for had not been granted. They wanted to believe in the Tsar as they had in the past, but he did not seem to care for his people. It was the turn of the century—a century which promised the people of most countries greater freedoms, but in Russia they looked forward to a bleak future. It was true that the new industrialization provided jobs in the cities, but conditions in the factories remained poor—long hours, small pay, dangerous working conditions. Without a voice these workers could do little to improve these conditions.

Groups of workers arrived daily to speak with Tolstoy about the situation. Many were bitter. Their loyalty to the Tsar was beginning to crumble. They longed for a better life. Tolstoy sensed the rebellious mood of the workers. Time and again he wrote to the Tsar and his ministers warning them of the people's discontent. But they did not respond and were irritated by his constant demands. To them, Tolstoy was a thorn in their side.

In 1902, against the Tsar's better judgment, the Holy Synod, as the governing body of the church of Russia was called, excommunicated Lev Nikolayevich Tolstoy. They charged him with writing articles against the church and believing in a form of religion not sanctioned by the mother church. It was obvious to everyone that this was the government's way of deflating Tolstoy's power. But their plan backfired. The public, already rebellious, reacted violently. They protested and rioted. Letters of support came in each mail. Even Sofya Andreyevna, a devout Orthodox Catholic who feared her husband would die without the proper funeral rites, wrote a passionate letter to the church.

A revolutionary mood hung over the Tolstoy house and infected Sasha. How could the church, which taught man to follow Christ's teachings, condemn a man who lived so strictly by them? The reason he did not go to church was that he felt the priests did not apply Christ's teachings to their everyday dealings with the masses. But he was religious in his own way—helping the people, living a pure life, praying to God directly. Surely such a life of dedication was not a crime. Fired with resentment, she and Tanya's stepson, Misha Sukhotin (who was staying with them), abandoned their studies and devoted themselves to distributing Tolstoy's letters to the Tsar and the Holy Synod. They copied each by hand and printed at the top REQUEST TO HAND ON! But they soon grew frustrated with their work. They could not possibly reach enough people in this way. The work was far too slow. What they needed was a printing press! Then they could copy Lev's banned articles over and over.

Misha discovered an old press and decided to smuggle it into the house after dark. That night Sasha could scarcely sit still. Every time she heard a loud noise she jumped, for it was against the law to have presses on private property. It was very late when Misha finally brought the forbidden machine into the house. Together the two young "revolutionaries" carried it through the pantry and into Misha's room. When everyone was in bed, Misha and Sasha began their work. The article had to be copied by hand in purple ink and then impressed on gelatine from which the printing would be done. It was messy work and they fumbled awkwardly with the ink and gel, but eventually they learned how to run it.

Night after night they worked at the press until someone spied on them and told Sofya Andreyevna. They were so carried away by the work that they never even heard her enter Misha's room.

"What are you doing here?" she asked in astonishment, looking at the paper-filled room.

"We—we were printing," Sasha replied nervously.

"What!"

"Printing."

Sasha and Misha tried to appear as casual as they could and explained how they could not remain indifferent to the general protest against the excommunication. They wanted to act. They wanted to spread the words and ideas of Lev Nikolayevich.

"How dare you bring a hectograph into the

house!" Sonya shouted. "It's prohibited. And what if they search the house and find this nasty business and all of us are put into prison because of you? What then?"

In the morning Misha took back the hectograph. Sasha was forbidden to enter his room for the rest of his stay. Lev Nikolayevich laughed on seeing their "edition" of his work and soon offered Sasha a more "suitable" job. With Tanya and Masha now gone he needed a new assistant. It was now clear to him that Sasha was his choice.

In the summer the family moved permanently back to Yasnaya Polyana. Now that there were no more boys to educate in Moscow and Sasha had elected to stop her studies, there was no reason to go back and forth with the seasons. Sasha had been preparing for an examination and was only a course away from taking it, but she no longer wanted to spend time taking classes. After all, this was where she had always wanted to be—at her father's side. At last she was there and she did not want anything or anyone to distract her.

7

AT FIRST SASHA FOUND HER NEW WORK DIFFICULT.
Her father's handwriting was nearly illegible and she
would often stay up half the night in despair, trying
to make out his words. She envied her sister Masha,
who seemed to have no trouble in deciphering his
scrawl and in copying his texts neatly. Sasha often
had to recopy her pages over and over before she was
satisfied that they were neat.

As she grew more adept at copying, Sasha realized
that she wanted to fully understand her father's
articles and books. She wanted to understand his
beliefs and why he had rejected his former life. So
she read his novels; she struggled to grasp his
religious and political articles; during dictation she
interrupted for him to explain a complicated point.
It was worth his annoyance for she wanted to
understand everything. And slowly she did.

The more she read the more she found herself
agreeing with her father's views. She too felt con-

tempt at the exploitation of the masses by the church and state. She too felt the need of constant striving for perfection and a total relationship with God. She too could see the futility of war and violence and the greater good of understanding and love. She knew in her heart that she fell short of her sisters in many ways. She wished she did not care what others thought or that she could deny herself physical comforts for the good of her soul.

While Sasha believed she could never achieve the goals dictated by her father's beliefs, she was nonetheless becoming fiercely dedicated to them. This dedication now filled her life. Many men tried to court her, for although she did not possess her mother's and sisters' good looks, at seventeen she had a newfound self-confidence and disarming frankness. But she was not interested in domestic things such as marriage and children. She had seen too closely the problems of a difficult marriage and the effects of a mother not able to give the love a child needed.

Having made her decision, Sasha refused each proposal she received. No, the only life she wanted was the one she had . . . working and caring for a great man—a man she believed rose above the ordinary and whose thoughts and deeds affected people throughout the world.

But Lev Nikolayevich Tolstoy was growing old. He was in his seventies.

In the summer he fell dangerously ill with pneumonia. Physicians insisted he travel south to Gaspra in the Crimea where the climate was dry. It was dangerous to move him in his weakened condition,

44

but the family obtained a private railway car for the long journey. Sasha, Masha, husband Nikolai, and Sofya Andreyevna went with him. The cook Semen Nikolayevich, the seamstress Olga, and the valet Ilya Vasilievich were to follow.

The train moved at a slow, easy pace. As the air grew warm and balmy outside, Sasha opened the railway carriage window. She and Masha gazed out at the countryside and marveled at the chalk hills, the white walls of the Ukrainian peasant huts, and the giant poplar trees that swayed in the light wind. Once in a while their father managed to raise himself to see the view, but it was not easy and he tired quickly.

The family planned to eat in the station restaurant at the next stop, but when they arrived the platform was filled with students. They terrified Sasha. Her father was in no condition to speak with them.

"Ask Lev Nikolayevich to come to the window!" they shouted. "We implore you! For just one minute!"

"But he cannot—he is not well. To speak with you would exhaust him," Sasha replied from the car.

But Lev Nikolayevich came to the window and tried to speak with his admirers. His voice was weak and trembled. "Hurrah," they shouted, taking off their caps and waving them. "Lev Nikolayevich! Good health!"

The train began to move. The excitement and the emotion had drained Sasha's father. But at each station crowds gathered and he rose and leaned against the window to greet them.

Once at Gaspra, his health began to improve. He was soon able to work again. But then in January he suffered a relapse and family members were summoned. Every night at least two would sit by his side. Masha, who was weak and ill herself, often stayed all night. Thoughts of death seemed to crowd their father's mind. He would often recite a poem he found amusing:

> Now the dear old man has begun to groan,
> Now the dear old man has begun to cough.
> It is time for the dear old man to get under his shroud,
> Under his shroud and into his grave.

Sasha did not enjoy her father's humor. She thought only of saving his life. Everyone feared death was near. No one, however, was ready to give him up to God.

But the crisis passed and eventually his health improved enough for him to be taken outside. It was Sasha's and Ilya Vasilievich's job to push him about in his makeshift wheelchair. The chair was heavy, and on an incline it was often hard to manage. It would pull both Sasha and Ilya along, so that their feet seemed to glide along the gravel path. Sasha's face often reflected terror, lest at any moment, everyone might fall over. But the occupant would shout out, "Courage, courage," and laugh as the vehicle sped along.

Just before the family was to return home, Sasha fell ill with fever and pains in her stomach. The doctors suspected a slight case of typhoid.

"We should have stayed at Yasnaya. It will be a miracle if we leave here alive. Lev Nikolayevich has been sick for months, then Masha and now Sasha!

We must leave quickly!" Sofya Andreyevna insisted.

As soon as the invalids were well enough to travel they started back to Yasnaya Polyana. Sasha had to be carried down the curving staircase to the carriage. On the train her father, who was weak and emaciated, came into her compartment and sat at her feet. "Do you need anything?" he asked her. It seemed odd to Sasha that she, always so healthy and strong, could not get up to help him, while he, so feeble and thin, was trying to help her.

Once home, Lev Nikolayevich and Sasha quickly recovered. The familiar environment seemed all the remedy they needed. Still, the entire family feared for his health and from then on, whenever he seemed to be having trouble breathing or looked pale, someone would grab his wrist and count his pulse.

When Sasha was not needed by her father, she was usually to be found with Dr. Nikitin, the physician who worked for the family in Gaspra. There was little for him to do now that his patients were all well. Sasha and he decided to open a dispensary for the peasants. Sasha furnished it with medical supplies and received patients, in exchange for some on-the-job training.

The whole village soon heard that a free dispensary had opened. The district zemstvo, which was an elected assembly, was responsible for roads, mail, elementary schools and medical help. But its dispensaries, like its schools, were few and the distances between them were great. Often it was impossible for a peasant to travel the distance when sick. So they flocked to this new dispensary. It was housed in a

47

vacant peasant izba and was furnished meagerly with wood benches and shelves, but everyone made do. The work was hard at first, for Sasha had never before seen the disease and misery that entered the dispensary each day. It was a new view of life, one filled with sorrow and poverty. She would never forget the peasants' faces as they looked up at her and the doctor so trustfully. In time the doctor left and the dispensary closed, but by then Sasha had discovered that there was room in her heart for both Lev Nikolayevich and the peasants. And she dreamed of the day she could open a bigger dispensary for the peasants of Yasnaya Polyana.

8

WHILE SASHA WAS BUSY WORKING IN DR. NIKITIN'S dispensary and thinking about how she could someday help the people of Yasnaya Polyana on a larger scale, events were taking place that would affect both Sasha's and the peasants' lives for some time to come.

During the family's stay in the Crimea, Nicholas II had been entertaining ideas of expanding Russia's political influence along his new railway through Manchuria. Nicholas was able to obtain a twenty-five-year lease of the southern part of the much prized Liatung Peninsula, including the city of Port Arthur, located at the tip of southern Manchuria. Control of this area insured influence over neighboring China and Korea and was a definite threat to nearby Japan's national security. The Japanese minister in St. Petersburg sought an immediate audience with the Tsar to discuss the situation. His efforts were denied. On February 3, 1904, the Japanese minister boarded a train for Japan. Five days later Japanese destroyers attacked Russian ships stationed at Port Arthur. Before the public had time to understand the significance of the attack, the Russo-Japanese War was declared. Peasants and workers across Russia immediately received draft notices.

Everywhere men resisted the draft. They did not understand why they suddenly had to fight in the Far East. Sasha's brother Andrei was drafted, as was the family cook, Semen Nikolayevich. In the village, unwilling men were dragged off to be soldiers. Distraught women crowded the Tolstoy house, begging and pleading for help. Many did not know how they would live without their husbands' or brothers' income.

Worst of all, daily reports came in of terrible Russian defeats. The death toll quickly climbed into the thousands. Whatever patriotism the peasants had now vanished. In its place grew shame and hostility at a humiliating war and the Tsar who caused it.

Sasha's father refused to take sides but was obviously disturbed by the fighting. "I am neither for Russia nor for Japan," he would say, "but for the working people of both countries who are deceived by their governments to go to war against their conscience, their religion, and their own God."

Sasha would watch as her father paced the room after reading the daily war reports. "Amazing," he said over and over. "Christianity forbids killing, and so does Buddhism. And yet here are two peoples professing religions which forbid killing that are hatefully killing, drowning, and maiming each other!"

He feared the approach of revolution. He felt the

temper of the workers, soldiers, and peasants from the conversations and endless letters that came to him from every corner of Russia. And he knew that the war with Japan was straining the people's patience to the utmost.

Tolstoy also received letters and visits from revolutionaries who were seizing this opportunity to turn the people against the Tsarist regime. They believed that Lev Tolstoy was one of them, since he had fought against the church and the Tsar for so long. They did not realize that he believed one government would be as evil as the next and that violence could never solve the people's woes.

At lunch one day Lev told Sasha about one such visit. "Oh, Lord," he said, shaking his head heavily. "It was horrible. 'You cannot improve the people's lot by violence,' I said. And the young man interrupted me and said, 'You are mistaken! Not that we cannot—we must! We must destroy without pity all those who exploit the people!' He was a schoolboy, about seventeen years old. What hatred! What hatred!" Sasha grew alarmed at her father's flushed face as he described the episode. She had never seen him so angry. "I began telling him of the law of God," he continued. "Of the teachings of Christ—'It's all foolishness,' he interrupted me, 'there is no God!'"

Sasha too was disturbed over the recent turn of events. The people were angry. They wanted rights and education and better living conditions. Their spirit had been pushed down for too long and finally the age-old hold of the Tsar on his people was beginning to loosen. The years of oppressive rule, the archaic class structure, and the unwanted war

51

seemed to guarantee revolution.

On Sunday, January 22, 1905, an organization of 120,000 workers with a priest at its head marched peacefully toward the Winter Palace in St. Petersburg. They were protesting working conditions in the cities and planned to present the Tsar with a petition. The marchers carried icons and crosses and portraits of the Tsar. Most felt confident that the Tsar was unaware of their discontent and would change the situation once he found out. But the Tsar was not even in the Winter Palace, and before anything could be discussed, the imperial troops were ordered to fire on the workers. As people, icons and portraits fell to the ground, marchers shouted, "The Tsar will not help!" In minutes hundreds lay dead. Bloody Sunday, January 22 was called, not only for the blood shed on that day, but for the blood that would be shed because of it.

The entire country reacted to the brutal slayings. Railroads were stalled, strikes were called, electricity and water were cut off. During the general strike workers in St. Petersburg organized a *soviet*, or council, to represent them in dealing with the imperial government. Fearfully, the government began to work out a constitution to pacify the people. In St. Petersburg, a man called Lenin stood on soapboxes and insisted the government's promises and plans were empty. Any Duma, or congress, the Tsar set up would undoubtedly be packed with his own men. Lenin spoke of his party, the Bolsheviks, and how they planned to overthrow the imperial regime and set up a government run by the workers—a communistic government. Such talk carried fresh tremors of discontent throughout central Russia. In the country peasants set manor houses on fire, murdered landlords, and stole property. *They will hang us from the nearest birch tree,* Sasha thought anxiously. But the peasants did not touch Yasnaya Polyana.

Then in May of 1905 came news of the loss of Russia's entire fleet. Soon after, the government issued a manifesto proclaiming a people's constitution and plans for the establishment of the congress or Duma in which the people would have a say in the running of the government. Sasha was in Tula on the day it was declared. Crowds everywhere shouted and blocked traffic. The streets were thick with police. But it was not clear to Sasha whether the people were rejoicing at the news or whether new disorders were about to flare up.

Elections to the new state Duma began. Slowly the furor died down. Many workers and peasants were not quite ready for Bolshevism and all-out revolution. Some wanted to give the new congress a chance, others had been loyal to aristocrats and were afraid they would be considered traitors, others simply did not want change.

The government began to gain the upper hand as the people hesitated. Small reactionary groups started to appear in the country. They were backed by the government and it was their job to create friction between the people . . . to set Jews against peasants, peasants against workers. With the people disunited and pacified by the weak Duma, the chances of revolution began to lessen. For the moment, the government felt secure. The birth of a son to the Tsar furthered their sense of security.

As the year drew to a close, Sasha turned her attention once more to working with the peasants. The parish and zemstvo schools in the district were few and were not very good. Most could not handle more than thirty children and usually boys were chosen over girls. Sasha decided to start a small school for girls where she could teach basic skills— reading, writing, and arithmetic. Few women in the village could write or read.

Each morning Sasha rose early, drank a cup of strong rye coffee and ran to the school. Her girls were always waiting. Together they built a fire in the small stove and settled down to their lessons. In the afternoon Sasha dedicated herself to working with her father. She had purchased a typewriter for the endless letters and articles she copied each day. When the school was in full operation and Sasha had gained confidence in her ability to tackle a number of jobs at once, she reopened the dispensary with the aid of the new doctor, Dushan Petrovich.

There was no time left for outside interests, but Sasha had never felt so useful and happy. She was content in the belief that she was doing meaningful work, her country was at peace, and Lev Niko- layevich Tolstoy needed and relied on her.

9

SASHA'S SENSE OF WELL-BEING LASTED FOR ONLY A short while. In August 1906 her mother suddenly took sick. A surgeon was brought in and he and Dushan Petrovich agreed that an operation was necessary.

Masha and Sasha nursed their mother each day. Her suffering was intense but she bore her pain well. As it grew so did her gentleness. She made every effort to save her family grief. She muffled her cries and smiled kindly at everyone's help. When Lev Nikolayevich came to her, she took his hand and whispered, "Forgive me, forgive me." Sasha suddenly realized that despite the hostility she bore her mother, she felt love as well. She looked into her eyes and the anger she had always felt seemed like a far-off nightmare.

Soon the surgeon's assistants and nurses arrived to prepare for the operation. They brought with them instruments and an operating table. Just before the operation Sonya requested a priest. Then she asked forgiveness of her children and the servants. Lev walked into the woods to be alone.

From her lookout on the stairs, Sasha could watch the preparations. She could see the operating table in the center of the room, its floor wet with antiseptic. The white-clad doctors moved about the room slowly. Then Sofya Andreyevna was carried in and the door was shut.

It seemed an interminable time before the door was reopened. But finally the surgeon, looking flushed and tired, walked out. Sasha searched his face for some sign. He nodded to her. The operation had been a success. Sasha rushed into the woods.

"Papa, it's all right!" she told her father breathlessly.

He waved her away and Sasha realized that he wanted to be alone.

As with Vanichka's death, Lev hoped that his wife's sufferings would bring about a reconciliation. Her new gentleness and kindness seemed to promise this. But he feared she would resume her old ways and the distance between them would increase once again. Indeed, as she grew strong, Sonya went back to being her old self. Disappointed, her husband began to avoid her. Arguments rang out daily from their room.

Sasha watched in pain as her parents fought and the unity they had shared in their moment of crisis vanished. With it also disappeared the feeling of closeness Sasha had felt for her mother. Sonya, feeling rejected once again, became cool and sharp with Sasha. Sasha meanwhile, feeling betrayed and confused, remained aloof. If her mother's love was to be fleeting, then so be it. At least her father loved her and needed her with him.

As if such emotion and upset wasn't enough for the Tolstoy family to bear, three months later they were given yet another heartache to deal with. Sweet Masha, always doing for others, always weak and frail, caught a cold which turned into pneumonia. Within days Sasha's sister was unrecognizable and could hardly speak. Day after day Sasha sat beside her, trying to make her comfortable. But she recognized the expression on her sister's face. She had seen it years before on little Vanichka. On the ninth day Masha's faltering breath simply stopped.

Sasha could not speak to anyone of Masha's death. But it was always with her. She felt deserted as she had when Vanichka had died. She found herself remembering her father's words, "He is not dead because we still love him and so he continues to live in us."

Sasha went back to teaching the village girls and working, but somehow everything had changed. Her enthusiasm was gone. Thoughts of Masha and the endless work she had done for the peasants crowded her mind. It seemed she could never achieve what her sister had in her short lifetime. Sasha felt that she would never be as well-loved or as devoted to the happiness of others. It didn't seem enough to run a small dispensary and a tiny school. One had to dedicate one's entire life to such things, and even then there was no accounting for the twists and turns life had in store.

Her father appeared equally unsettled about life

and the future. Since the 1905 revolution, many of his followers had drifted away from his philosophies. The present current of active revolution had seized them and they could no longer be satisfied to wait for a gradual change in government. The loss of so many followers and his daughter made life at Yasnaya Polyana more difficult than ever. The idea of retreating to a quiet place where he could meditate on life and death grew ever more appealing. It was only a matter of time before he would come to the realization that he must leave his family and Yasnaya Polyana. It was a decision Sasha had feared, perhaps had dreaded, since she was a small girl. But it was one she understood and would even support if she had to—come what may.

10

SASHA WAS SOUND ASLEEP WHEN A LOUD KNOCKING at her door awakened her. Fearfully, she jumped out of bed and asked who was there. "I am leaving immediately," her father's anxious voice replied. Sasha opened the door. Her father stood there, a candle burning in his hand, casting light on his fully clothed figure. "I am leaving for good. Help me pack," he whispered.

Sasha quickly dressed and joined Varya, her mother's typist, and Dushan Petrovich, who were already packing for her father's departure. Together they packed books, medical supplies, and clothing.

"You stay here, Sasha," her father told her. "I shall send for you in several days, when I decide where I am going . . . perhaps to the monastery near Shamordino, where my sister lives."

Sasha nodded. His sister, Marya Nikolayevna, was a nun who lived in a convent in Shamordino. With every passing moment her father grew more agitated. Sasha fumbled with straps, valises would not shut. The entire episode seemed like a strange dream. She could not help but wonder if her father would appear at his study door as always in the morning.

Finally all was ready and he went out to the stable to fetch the carriage. In moments he was back, his cap gone, his clothes filthy. Sasha looked at the pitiful sight. It was foggy out and he had fallen in his agitated excitement. He got a lamp and went off to the stable once more. Sasha could see that he was shaken. Disturbed, she carried the boxes and valises out front.

Suddenly everything was in the carriage and her father sat, alongside Dushan, ready to leave. The stable boy jumped onto his horse, a burning torch in one hand, and cried "Drive on!" to horse and footman. Sasha's insides started to churn. "No!" she said quietly, and jumped onto the carriage and, leaning into it, reached for her father's hand. "We'll see each other soon. Good-bye, darling," he said.

Then the carriage was moving and all that could be seen was the dwindling light of the stable boy's torch.

Sasha went back into the house. It was sometime after five, three hours before the train left. She sat in her father's armchair, not knowing if she was shivering from fear or chill. At eight o'clock she finally got up and walked about the house. Many of the servants had already noticed their master's absence and were whispering about the news.

Sofya Andreyevna did not awaken till eleven. She had been up late the night before and Lev Nikolayevich had caught her rummaging in his papers. Her illness had grown worse of late and she was forever fretting and fussing about a conspiracy she felt was afoot. And not without good reason. Tolstoy had recently signed a will which left everything in Sasha's hands. It took away control of the monies Sonya had always depended upon. In the will Sasha was instructed to buy up the lands from her mother and siblings and finally turn them over to the peasants.

"Where's Papa?" Sonya asked her daughter.

"He's gone away," Sasha said firmly.

"Where?"

"I do not know," Sasha answered and handed her mother the letter he had left for his wife. Her hands trembled as she read it:

> My departure will distress you and I regret this, but you must understand and believe that I could not act otherwise. My situation was getting, did get, intolerable. In addition to everything else, I cannot live any longer in such circumstances of luxury as those in which I have been living and I am doing what old men of my years do—they withdraw from worldly life to live in solitude and quiet for the last days of their lives. Please do not come after me if you discover where I am. Your coming would only worsen my and your situation. It cannot alter my decision . . .

"He's gone, he's gone for good!" Sofya Andreyevna cried, not even finishing the letter. "Goodbye, Sasha. I'm going to drown myself!" Sonya rushed out of the house. Sasha and a Tolstoyan who was nearby ran after her. Sasha reached the platform just as her mother slipped on its wet planks into the icy water. Sasha jumped in and caught her by the edge of her dress. Together, the Tolstoyan and Sasha managed to lift the crazed woman out of the river.

Sasha watched over her mother all day long. She sent telegrams to her sister and brothers explaining what had happened and asking them to come. When they arrived they immediately split into two camps: those who felt their father should have stayed with their mother, that as a Christian he should have borne his "cross" to the end; and those who felt he had to leave for his own sake.

Only Sasha knew for sure where her father was, but the family soon guessed. Worried that his plans would be thwarted, Sasha left for Shamordino. By the time she reached the village, her father had already arranged to rent a small cottage near the convent and monastery. Sasha's news so upset him that he decided to leave the next day. He did not even wait to say good-bye to his sister.

But Lev Nikolayevich could not find safety. On board the train he was immediately recognized. It was not long before the entire crew and all the passengers learned of his presence. As they pushed into his compartment to see him, he grew more and more agitated. By afternoon he had a fever and complained of feeling ill. Sasha was close to despair. They were on a stuffy train, bound for she knew not where. *Where are we going? Where is home? What am I doing?* she asked herself miserably. Her father looked so frail and helpless. He was old and ill and in need of care. But they could not go back.

When the train pulled into the brightly lit station of Astapova the feeble Tolstoy got off. He was simply too ill to continue. There was no hotel in the small town but the stationmaster, like the others, recognized the famous old man and kindly offered his own home. Together, they put Lev Nikolayevich to bed. Before long, he fell into a deep faint. Sasha cabled her brother Sergei to send doctors. When they arrived they diagnosed pneumonia.

Meanwhile, Sofya Andreyevna—beside herself with grief—had ordered a special train and was bound for Astapova with Andrei, Misha, Tanya, a doctor, and a nurse. By the time they arrived the small town had become the center of activity. The news of Tolstoy's illness had spread rapidly. Telegrams were sent throughout the world. Newspapermen and photographers had flocked to the stationmaster's house. Crowds waited outside for news of their hero's health.

But Lev Nikolayevich had no idea that all this was going on outside. He did not know that his wife of forty-eight years, from whom he had fled in the night, was within calling distance. The family had decided not to let her into the sickroom for fear her presence would aggravate his condition. So she wandered about the village aimlessly; she spoke thoughtlessly with reporters and newsmen; she peered pathetically into the stationmaster's windows, desperate for a glimpse of her husband. Within, he grew progressively worse.

"On Sonya, on Sonya much is falling," he whispered. "We have arranged things badly." Then to Sasha he said, "I want to advise you that there are many people in the world besides Lev Tolstoy." These were the last words he spoke to Sasha.

When it was clear Lev was growing much worse, the family allowed Sofya Andreyevna into the sickroom. She knelt by her husband's bed and whispered words of endearment. But he did not hear them. He died without ever knowing she was there.

Two days later a train carried a plain coffin to Yasnaya Polyana. Thousands waited at the station platform. A group of peasants carried a banner that read: Lev Nikolayevich—the memory of your kindness will not die among us orphan peasants of Yasnaya Polyana.

Sasha, too, felt like an orphan. Her father's love and work had meant everything to her. She now felt empty, alone. "There are many people in the world besides Lev Tolstoy," her father had told her, but after his death it was difficult to care about anything or anyone. It seemed to Sasha that her life had been a series of tragedies and now she could not extricate herself from the sadness of them.

She could not have known in 1910 that her life so far was merely a preparation for the incredible events that were about to take place and the mammoth work that was to be hers. Nor could she have known that in the historic years to come thousands of people would look to Alexandra Lvovna Tolstoy for aid as they had once her celebrated father.

PART TWO

Alexandra Lvovna

11

A GLOOM HUNG OVER YASNAYA POLYANA AFTER Lev Nikolayevich Tolstoy's death. The peasants in the village spoke in whispers about the man most had known since their birth. He had left an indelible impression on each of their lives and few would ever forget him. In the old main house the servants also spoke in whispers, for Sofya Andreyevna was often not well. She spent much of her days sitting in her husband's armchair thinking about the man whom she had loved and fought with for forty-eight years. After his death there had been great bitterness among her children. Sasha had been made executrix of her father's will and she had, according to his wishes, turned over much of the land to the peasants. So heated were the arguments over this that Sasha decided to leave the house in which she had been brought up. She purchased a small estate in Novaia Polyana, three miles away, and moved out.

Sasha's days were now filled with looking after her

new home; buying purebred horses she hoped to train and ride, and cattle whose milk she sent daily to the hospital in Tula; and working with the peasants to improve their crop yield. In winter she went to Moscow to organize her father's papers and prepare them for publication. Her life was active but it lacked a central person or cause to be dedicated to. Oddly enough, a crime in the Balkans provided her with one.

The Balkans was an area in southeastern Europe which included the states of Bosnia, Serbia, Montenegro, Rumania, Bulgaria, and Albania. It had long been a region of tremendous internal and international strife stemming from outside desires for political influence and internal struggles for greater freedoms. One group fighting for these internal freedoms were the Slavs—a people related to the Russians who resented their Austro-Hungarian rulers and wanted to join with Serbia, a free Slav nation.

On June 18, 1914, Archduke Franz Ferdinand, heir to the Austro-Hungarian Empire, was shot to death in Sarajevo, Bosnia—a pocket of Slavic unrest. The Austro-Hungarians declared war on Serbia where the murderers were being sheltered. They were backed by a land-hungry Germany who had long rivaled Russia for political influence in the Balkans. On August 1, 1914, Germany declared war on Russia. With a sudden surge of loyalty to his Slavic cousins, Nicholas changed the name of his capital from the Germanic "St. Petersburg" to the Slavic "Petrograd" and went to war. An ally, France was compelled to follow suit. When Germany threatened neutral Belgium, her ally, England, entered the war. In time Turkey joined Austria and Germany. Like dominoes, the western and eastern European nations one by one took up arms. And for the first time in history a world war was under way.

Curiously, after so many years of internal turmoil, the war at first unified the Russian people. They rallied behind the Tsar. Suddenly, differences in belief and status did not matter. Later, when the war dragged on and claimed millions of lives, resentment would build as it had during the Japanese war. And once again the revolutionaries would turn the tide to their advantage. But for now Russians were unified and they eagerly traded their farming tools or factory wages for guns.

Sasha immediately decided to join the war effort as a nurse. She lost no time in confronting her mother with her decision.

"Why do you want to go to war?" Sofya Andreyevna asked her quietly. "There is no point to it. Your father was against war, and now you want to take part in it."

Sasha looked at her aging mother impatiently. "I don't think he was against my doing God's work by helping the sick and wounded," she replied firmly—defiantly.

"Well, I gave you my opinion, but I know it is useless. You always have your way," her mother quipped back.

Sasha began taking nursing courses and soon joined a hospital where she could get practical experience. It was hard work and at times deeply disturbing. The sight of naked men embarrassed her, an open wound revolted her. But the shock and embarrassment gradually vanished as she realized that someone in pain was in need of her help.

War had not been her father's way. But then, all his words had not prevented it. It seemed that nothing or no one could stop the war now, nor the pain it was bound to create. Perhaps by being qualified—and by being there—she could ease its sting.

12

SASHA'S FIRST POST WAS IN TURKEY ON THE BANKS of the Euphrates River. The work was difficult and draining. The Turks used dum-dum bullets which caused gaping wounds in their victims. The doctors in her unit performed amputation after amputation.

Each day soldiers asked her over and over, "Have they left the leg? Where is my arm? I don't feel anything!" Sasha tried to answer their questions and comfort the soldiers. But often, looking into their young faces, it was difficult to keep from breaking down. Their loss seemed to point acutely to the waste and futility of war.

"Sister," a handsome Cossack sobbed when Sasha admitted his leg had been removed. "What can I do now? My Dunya, my sweet, sweet Dunya, she won't love a cripple. She will leave me!"

Sasha looked into the young man's eyes and groped for his hand to hold. "If your Dunya is worth anything she'll love and care for you even more." She prayed that night that the Cossack's Dunya truly would.

From the small settlement the detachment traveled by horse to Turkish Armenia, their supplies strapped to the backs of camels. They traveled for months in this manner—sometimes to set up a hospital, sometimes a first-aid camp. They journeyed through deep snow, their legs constantly sore and their supplies usually low. Often they found themselves nursing diseased more than war-wounded, for an epidemic of typhoid had broken out throughout the region.

Sasha began to look more like a Russian peasant woman or a young Cossack boy than the "countess" she now was. Her gray coat was forever soaked in horse sweat, her loose Turkish trousers were thinned from rubbing against the horse's back each day, a gun was always strapped to her waist in case of attack. Traveling this way, constantly battling disease with never enough to eat, began to wear Sasha and her aides down. One after another they became ill themselves. Eventually Sasha's resources wore down too and she contracted malaria. After the illness ran its course she was sent home for a rest.

Forty pounds lighter, looking ten years older, Sasha found it difficult to rest or remain inactive. She could think of little other than the war and the political situation that caused it. She pored over newspapers. They were filled with talk of defeat and the ongoing costs of the war, whose end was not in sight. From neighbors she learned of rumors about the Tsarina Alexandra and her growing dependence on a strange unkempt mystic by the name of Rasputin. It seemed her son, Alexis, suffered from a disease called hemophilia and she had gone to Rasputin for help. He had some success and she now relied on him heavily. Some said that it was he who actually ruled the government while Nicholas spent his time at army headquarters. Whatever the case, the mood was openly hostile and revolutionaries everywhere seized the opportunity to point to Rasputin's power as a symbol of the monarchy's collapse.

Sasha was anxious to return to the front. The overall mood frightened her. It seemed that revolution was close. The people had stood behind the Tsar one last time and he had failed. The revolutionaries would not let the power slip from their hands again. More blood would be shed, of that she was positive.

Her superiors did not lose time in sending Sasha back to the front. Her reputation as a highly efficient, dedicated worker was well known. Her superiors had received report after report commending her on her bravery and her skill at teaching others. Now they transferred her from the Turkish to the western front. Her first task was to organize a medical detachment and three mobile units. The object of the detachment was to set up stationary hospitals near battles while mobile units went right onto the battlefield. She had ten days to organize her first assignment. She stocked the detachment with provisions, arranged for staff, cars, and horses and was on the road in nine.

The detachment moved from battle to battle and gradually grew used to the extreme conditions under which they had to work. Everyone was on edge, there was never any time to relax or think about what was happening. The noise, the pressure, and the bloodshed were constant.

One night the sound of German planes droned overhead. Bombs suddenly went off around the detachment. Everyone started to panic. Orderlies began to run out of the makeshift hospital toward underground shelters . . . leaving their injured behind. Sasha could not believe her eyes. She tried to scream to them but could not speak. Then she found her voice: "Where are you going?" she shrieked furiously. "Abandoning the sick? Come back, you scoundrels!" she cried, waving her gun at them. Meekly they returned to their posts. But a week later, when Sasha was in the nearest village, there was another attack. Seven of the fearful orderlies were killed running for cover.

Shortly thereafter Sasha was ordered to move the entire detachment to Smorgony. There was to be a major German-Russian battle nearby. The hospital was set up in the city and the mobile units, one of which was to be led by Sasha, would service the battle.

On the day of the battle, Sasha was instructed to set up beds in a shelter near the battlefield. She approached the shelter cautiously. Two German "sausages"—observation balloons—hung in midair not far off. The Germans were uncomfortably close! Sasha and her crew knelt down behind a hill and waited. Finally a soldier tapped her on the shoulder. She jumped. "Your excellency," the soldier whispered. "His excellency, the general, requests your presence. Follow me."

Sasha signaled for all but three of her unit to follow. They would remain outside with the horses.

Sasha scrambled down the hill and into the camouflaged shelter entrance. She and her assistants walked along a lengthy passage. Finally they came to a general who sat at a small table covered with papers. He showed Sasha where to set up the beds. Then he turned to her and said, "By the way, do you know where we are? Under the Germans . . ."

Sasha looked up, alarmed. "What? There are Germans above us? Are we that far underground?"

"Yes," he replied, smiling.

"Well, I certainly hope the ground is firm!"

At two in the morning they heard the sound of shells going off. The shells gave off a curious yellow smoke. The smoke gradually spread along the passage and into the shelter. It smelled like chlorine gas. "MASKS!" someone yelled. "MASKS!"

The deadly gas filled the shelter within a half hour. Suddenly Sasha remembered her three orderlies outside—without gas masks. She grabbed some extras lying on a nearby cot and darted for the entrance. Two muzzled young men from her detachment grabbed them from her and ran outside before she could object. Like all the members of her group, they preferred to risk their lives rather than hers.

The wounded began to pour in. People were screaming and the air was so thick and the noise so loud Sasha likened it in her mind to hell. Everyone worked feverishly. No one had ever treated poison-gas victims before. This was a new kind of warfare. A vicious, terrible kind. Everyone was choking and coughing from lack of breath.

At dawn when the battle neared its end and the air began to clear, Sasha asked a driver to take her by automobile back to her detachment. She would have to find out about her other two mobile units later.

As they drove, Sasha stared out the car window. She could see villagers lying in the fields, their faces purple from suffocation. *So this is chemical warfare,* she thought sadly. *What next?* Just then a sharp piercing sound came from overhead. The driver swerved the car away from the sound. It jerked from the sudden motion and then stopped. The driver lay unconscious over the steering wheel. At first Sasha thought he had been shot. But then she realized that he had hit his head on the wheel when the car stopped. Certain that they would be killed by a second shell momentarily, and not knowing how to drive herself, Sasha quickly crossed herself, looked toward heaven for forgiveness, and began to bang the driver with all her might. Everything depended on rousing him. Beside herself, she slapped his face. He began to come to. Apologizing profusely, she urged him to drive on.

They arrived at the hospital safely. She immediately ushered the driver into an examination room. The hospital had seen its share of action. Gassed soldiers and civilians filled the makeshift wards. Sasha made sure everything was in order, checked on her driver and finally went back to her little sleeping hut. Her legs were so swollen that she had to cut her shoes from her feet.

A week later she was presented with one of Russia's highest awards for bravery, the Medal of St. George.

13

IN MARCH OF 1917 SASHA AWOKE IN A HOSPITAL bed in Minsk, the largest town behind the western lines. She could not remember when she had fallen ill nor how long she had lain in bed. She scanned the large white room to get her bearings . . . a clock, the familiar smell of disinfectant, a woman coughing.

"It's come at last!" someone, out of view, was saying. "They've taken Petrograd and a provisional government has been set up. They say the Tsar has abdicated for both himself and his son, and his brother, the Grand Duke, has refused the throne as well!"

Sasha lay silent, not certain whether or not she was still in some feverish dream. Suddenly the face of a white-haired doctor appeared before her. It smiled.

"Ah, Comrade Tolstoy. You have been suffering from an acute infection. I am glad to see you with us at last."

Comrade—the word rang in her ears. So the revolution had come. No more "countess" or "excellency." She wasn't surprised. The men back at camp had been terribly irritable and resentful of late.

Since Smorgony, Sasha and her detachment had served in numerous battles. A few had gone well for the Russians, but more had ended in humiliating defeat. In Europe the war was not going well either. Germany seemed on the verge of victory. It was said that they planned an attack on Petrograd. Everywhere morale was low.

At the root of the problem was the Empress. She had never been well liked and the situation with Rasputin had added fuel to the fire. There were rumors that she was a German spy. Such talk weakened the Tsar's hold on his people. Never had the Russian people's respect for their Tsar and his ability been so low.

Although the Tsar refused to see the nation's growing hostility toward his wife and Rasputin, or the weakening effect it was having on the country, there were those who did. Many of his ministers tried to warn Nicholas. Even the Duma members tried to impress the Tsar with the seriousness of the situation. But Nicholas believed that the war had to be his first priority. Once it was won, then he could think about internal affairs.

But Rasputin's presence deepened the wound each day. Many members of the aristocracy were convinced the monk had to be removed in order to save the monarchy. Accordingly, three monarchists planned and carried out the cold-blooded murder of Rasputin. But their loyal effort proved in vain. By that time the seeds of revolution were sown.

Many demanded the execution of Alexandra. The people accused her of treason. In the cities poor living conditions heightened their discontent. Food trains had been rerouted by the Tsar to carry supplies and arms to the front. People were hungry, sickness was widespread. Women stood in lines waiting for daily rations of bread. In Petrograd the weather reached a record-breaking thirty-five degrees below zero for March. A fuel shortage, also caused by the war, had closed down factories. Out-of-work workers milled about the streets with nothing to do and no money or food to take home. Anger at the Tsar and his Tsarina, who lived in splendor while they suffered, welled up in the people's hearts. Suddenly—spontaneously— it burst forth. Everyone began to rebel. Women broke into bakeries, workers marched on government buildings insisting the Duma take over its management, Tsarist troops turned on their commanders and joined the "glorious revolution."

In days the people wrenched the city of Petrograd from the Tsar. It now belonged to them. The Tsar's cabinet of ministers had no alternative but to resign. The Duma set up an emergency Provisional Government. Their popular member, Kerensky, was selected president. Kerensky immediately realized that the only way the "people's revolution" could succeed and a social democracy be set up was if the Tsar resigned. If he remained in power, loyalties would conflict and the country would be pulled apart by civil war. The Tsar, realizing this to be true, abdicated for both himself and his ailing son, Alexis. Kerensky took the royal family into immediate

Friends and family at Yasnaya Polyana in 1906 (Sasha is second from left).

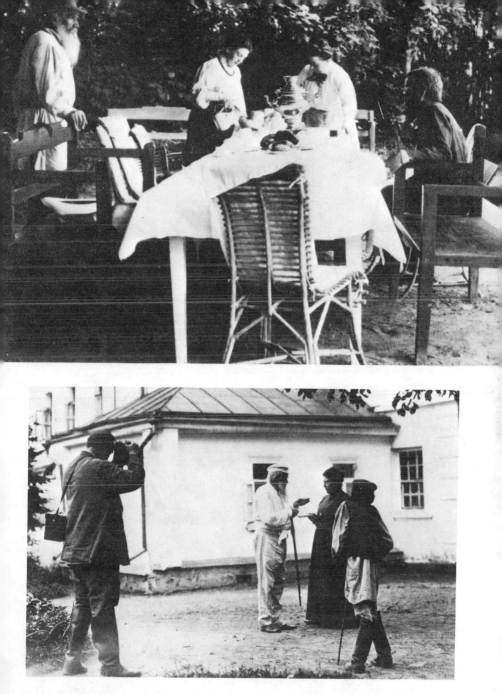

Above: Sasha pouring tea for her father and some Tolstoyans in 1907.
Below: Sasha and Tolstoy in front of the main house.

Facing page, above: Father and daughter in 1909.
Facing page, below: Tolstoy's study.
Above: Tolstoy's funeral procession in November, 1910.

Sasha Tolstoy in America in 1953.

Sasha at ninety in 1977.

custody and planned to find a way to send them safely out of the country.

The Provisional Government wanted democracy and freedom in Russia. Many liberals, including Sasha, genuinely hoped it would succeed. Here was a government that was working toward religious and social freedoms. But it misjudged the mood of the people. It continued the war when the people wanted it stopped, it did not give the peasants the land they had wanted for centuries and it did not improve the failing economy. And from the start it had a serious rival—the Petrograd Soviet of Workers' and Soldiers' Deputies, a council of soldiers and workers based on the Soviet of 1905. The Soviet had great influence over the workers and the garrison in Petrograd, and so was a serious power to be reckoned with. What is more, Soviets began to form throughout Russia, and in June they formed a Congress consisting of social-ists and Bolsheviks. This Congress elected an execu-tive committee which became the Supreme Soviet body. In essence, they had organized an alternative government.

To make matters worse, Lenin, who had been in exile in Switzerland, returned to Petrograd in April. He immediately roused the people and the Soviets with talk of all-out revolution. He demanded the seizure of land by the peasants and the takeover of factories by the workers, calling for "all power to the Soviets." His government would be a government run by the proletariat—the working people. Lenin's ideas were appealing to people who were tired of war, starvation, land debts, and lack of education and freedoms. His supporters grew. Soon everyone was calling for the overthrow of the nobility, the bourgeoisie—as they called all who owned land or were capitalists—and the church, whose teachings of blind faith in God the Communists believed dulled the actions of the people. It was a new age, one in which every worker should receive his share for his work, where everyone should have a say in government, where all profit should be recycled into the system, where everyone should work for a common goal—perfect communism.

Sasha did not know what to make of the situation. It had happened so quickly. Her head was spinning with questions. What about the war? What about her home and family? As soon as she was fit, she left for the front. There she found signs of revolution too. Generals were being addressed as "mister"; their orders were not being obeyed. Soldiers were fraternizing with the enemy; some were deserting openly.

It was obvious to Sasha that the Russian front was crumbling. Lenin promised peace and that was what everyone wanted. What price that peace would cost them, she did not know. There was no point in trying to keep the detachment going. All discipline had vanished. She gave up her post and headed for Moscow. With talk of the destruction of the aristocracy in the air, her main concern now was to see that the family, Yasnaya Polyana, and her own Novaia Polyana were safe.

But getting back to Moscow was no easy matter. Trains were still scarce and there was no organization. Sasha managed to find a seat near some loud soldiers who spent the long journey trying to throw "aristocrats" off the train. She took a deep breath, pulled out her small kettle, and offered the soldiers tea. If she could not beat them, she would have to join them . . . at least for now.

14

By the time Sasha arrived in Moscow in late 1917 the Provisional Government had fallen. In September Lenin's Bolshevik party had captured a majority vote in both the Petrograd and Moscow Soviets. On October 25 Bolshevik (Red) troops made up of workers, sailors and soldiers occupied Petrograd. On October 26 they attacked Provisional Government's headquarters and arrested many of its members. "The Great October Revolution" had succeeded. A "Soviet" government was set up in Petrograd with Comrade Lenin at its head.

Sasha was shocked by the Muscovites. They didn't seem disturbed by the change of government. In fact they seemed numbed by the rapid change of events. She assumed they simply did not want to think about the situation or its consequences. Few actually believed that Lenin or his Bolsheviks would stay in power any longer than Kerensky had. Even Lenin himself wasn't sure of his power. That was why it was so necessary for him to destroy his opposition and rapidly change the country over to his policies. And so the government allowed the peasants to seize land; it took control of the factories and transferred it to the Soviets; it nationalized all banks and took over private accounts. Soviet authorities assumed control over housing and food. Those who belonged to the upper and middle classes often lost their property and were looked upon with suspicion. All church property was seized and religious teaching in schools was forbidden.

It was not long before Sasha found out personally what nationalization meant. All her savings were taken over by the government. Nothing was left. She had no idea how she would live. For the moment she could live in Moscow at the house in Khamovniki Street, although most of the furniture and personal items had been stolen. But she would have to find smaller lodgings. It would be impossible to live in such a house without arousing the suspicions of the local authorities. As soon as she returned from the country she would start looking for work and lodgings. But first she had to go home.

Sasha did not look forward to the trip. As the railway tracks were in bad repair, the few trains running were always packed. One was lucky to get standing room on a cattle or coal freight. With the food shortage and free travel, everyone wanted to go south where food was still available. There they could trade clothes and soap for flour and sugar.

Sasha stood on the crowded platform for hours. Finally a southbound train arrived. Thousands stormed the waiting vehicle. Sasha took a deep breath, clutched her valise and moved forward. Someone yelled for her to stop shoving, but before she could answer back they were carried off by the crowd. Once in, Sasha tried to make herself as small as possible. It would be hard to stand like this, packed in for twenty hours. At least one could lean on one's neighbors without their complaining.

Sasha arrived at the station only to find out that her little house at Novaia Polyana was about to be taken from her. The entire contents, including the animals, were to be given over to the local Soviet. She rushed straight to the house. All her keepsakes were gone. Only the machinery, tools, and some of the furniture were left and they were to be relocated shortly. Sasha sat down on the bare floor. She felt totally defeated. Her two Eskimo dogs bounded up to her, licking her hands frantically. But even they could not cheer her up. She wanted new freedoms for the peasants. She, of all people, had worked for that goal. But the Bolsheviks wanted violent, godless change. They spoke of the equality of the individual but they did not consider that individual. The fact that one had been dedicated to a cause seemed to matter little if one had been born to the upper class. Sasha was thirty-two years old and there seemed to be no place for her in this frightening new world. Still, of one thing she was sure. She was not going to let the Soviet have her animals. She had heard rumors of how the peasants mistreated purebreds, not knowing what to do with them . . . killing them when they proved no good for farming. No, they could take everything from her but she was going to see to it that her animals were spared.

Sasha called the estate manager. A tall, dark Ukrainian man appeared.

"Harness the horses to the carts," she told him.

He did not move.

"Harness the horses," she repeated, her face growing flushed.

"But may we?" her former employee asked.

"But may we what?"

"The village Soviet forbade anyone taking anything away."

Sasha looked at the man in frustration. No one was willing to take matters into his own hands. "It's not your business to argue," she said firmly. "Harness up, I'll take responsibility for whatever happens."

They loaded the carts with the remaining machinery and furniture and drove over to Yasnaya Polyana where she placed them in an old shed. As soon as the carts were unloaded, they drove back to Novaia Polyana for more.

That evening Sasha napped in her now empty house on a pile of hay. It was not the way she had anticipated spending her first night home. Still, she had to do what she had to do. At three a.m. when it was still dark, she got up and took her thoroughbred horses to the market and sold them for half their worth to a villager she knew and trusted. In the morning she went to the Department of Agriculture in Tula and arranged to turn her cows over to them. At least they would be properly taken care of.

With her mission accomplished, Sasha mounted

the one horse she had not sold and with her two dogs running behind rode all the way back to Yasnaya Polyana.

Only her mother, her sister and her aunt Tanya Kuzminsky, who used to spend summers at Yasnaya Polyana, were there. All the servants save Ilya Vasilievich, the old valet, had deserted. He continued to serve the "countess" and never failed to come to the table with tattered but clean white gloves.

Sasha found that her fears about the safety of the estate had nearly come to pass. In late summer, peasants and Red soldiers had gone through the region stealing from manor houses and setting torches to them. Sofya Andreyevna and Tanya had telegraphed Kerensky and pleaded for him to send soldiers to preserve Tolstoy's home. Then they had packed up Lev's manuscripts and the family belongings and waited for the rioters to come. But they did not. They were met by villagers carrying pitchforks and axes. Kerensky, despite the fact that his Provisional Government was falling, managed to send one hundred soldiers. Between the villagers and Kerensky's soldiers Yasnaya Polyana and its inhabitants remained safe. But now Kerensky was no longer in power and everyone in the Tolstoy house wondered anxiously about the future.

Four months after Sasha's homecoming she read that Lenin had signed a peace treaty with Germany. He gave up huge tracts of Russian territory without a twinge of shame or regret. She wondered why the war had been fought. Why had all those boys in the trenches lost their limbs and their lives? Certainly not to gain international stature. Certainly not to enlarge Russia's dominions. She hoped that it had not all been in vain . . . and that the Russian Revolution which had finally come because of it, would prove to truly benefit the country and her countrymen.

15

On July 16, 1919, the imperial family was moved to the distant Ural Mountains. They were taken to a cramped basement cell and shot to death.

Two days after the royal family's murder, the Allies, consisting of France, Britain, and America, started a campaign to end the war. By November Austria and Germany sued for peace. By that time the death toll listed eight million killed and an even greater number permanently disabled. Gone was the affluence and prosperity Europe had enjoyed before the war. In its place were hunger and disease. Whole empires were destroyed. A new map had to be created. Austria's empire was gone. Two Slavic nations, Yugoslavia and Czechoslovakia, were created. A League of Nations, dedicated to preserving peace, would soon meet.

In Russia Lenin quickly moved to secure his power. The death of Nicholas and his heir was the first step, nationalization of the banks and the factories had been the second, and the nationalization of the great estates would be the third. By taking over the estates, Lenin sought to destroy whatever influence the old families might still have over loyal peasants.

Yasnaya Polyana was not spared. It was declared a state farm. The family was told that they could live in a small portion of the main house. A government official was placed in the house to oversee its operation. All house activities had to be cleared through him.

Sasha's situation in Moscow was not much better. She was able to find a nationalized apartment consisting of two tiny rooms. But she did not have enough food or fuel to live on. She was given a food card by the government, but her ration of a pound of bread each day, one pound of oil each month and a few pounds of cereal was simply not enough to survive on. A flourishing trade system had developed throughout the country since money was now worthless. Sasha soon found that the only way to get food was by trading. It was not long before she found herself crouched against a wall, her old jewelry, pots, pans, and clothes spread out on the sidewalk of an open-air market.

"How much for the necklace?" someone would ask.

"If you give me flour or bacon," she'd reply smoothly, "I'll make it cheaper, but for money—no." What was the good of money when there was nothing to buy?

When it grew dark and it was obvious nothing else could be sold, Sasha threw her things into a knapsack and carried them home on her back.

At night she prepared her dinner of cereal and

carrot or cabbage soup in what she liked to called her "magic" box. Each night she heated her dinner on the stove until it came to a boil. The she would place it, well covered, into the wooden box whose double sides were lined with burning shavings. Then she waited two hours. The heat within the box would steam her food without fuel or fire and she had only used her stove for a few minutes rather than two hours.

Sometimes she and a friend from her building would make soup and take it to the Red soldiers stationed all about the city. The men invariably stood close to a large fire, with a nice pile of lumber at their side. Usually they could be cajoled into trading a log or two for the homemade soup. In this way Sasha was guaranteed a few days' warmth and enough fuel to boil her dinner.

Once a month Sasha traveled to Yasnaya Polyana to see her mother, aunt, and sister. It was on one of these visits that she found her mother standing in the chill air washing windows and putting up huge winter frames. It seemed the government official thought little of putting elderly women to work. Sasha was furious. This was one indignity too many.

On her return to Moscow, Sasha went straight to the commissar of education. She pleaded that the estate be turned into a Tolstoy museum, with a library and model school. Sasha left his office the new "commissar of Yasnaya Polyana." Dreams that she had not thought of since her father's death now came to mind. Perhaps she would be able to work within this new system after all.

Sasha immediately fired the hated official at

Yasnaya Polyana. It would take a long time to achieve her goal. She would have to spend winters in Moscow, collecting materials for the museum. In the spring and summer she could work at Yasnaya Polyana on the library and school.

All spring and summer Sasha stayed in the country. Everything went according to schedule. She planned to leave for Moscow on November first by the midnight train.

The evening of her departure, Sasha finished packing her valises and went upstairs to have tea. It was a bitter night and her mother went to bed with a chill. Sasha's aunt sat at a small table by an inside wall playing solitaire, two shawls wrapped about her lean figure. The wind howled outside and rapped noisily on the windowpanes.

Sasha moved close to her aunt. "Auntie," she said, her broad face lighting up at a sudden thought. "Tell me a fortune." She was pleased that her aunt's new pastime could provide them both with some entertainment on this dreary night.

Her aunt finished her game and shuffled the cards. "All right," she replied, handing the cards to Sasha to cut. Then she spread them out before her. The only sound in the room was the wind and the samovar boiling in the corner. "Bad, very bad," the old woman said and swept the cards together in a swift movement with her gloved hands.

Sasha looked at her aunt questioningly. "What is it, Auntie? Tell me."

Her aunt shook her head and pulled her shawls close about her. "You can't always believe the cards," she said.

Curious, Sasha persisted. Finally her aunt said, "Illness and death of a close relative. You won't be going away tonight."

Sasha tried to make light of it. After all, her aunt was an old lady and it was gloomy out. But somehow she could not.

Sasha leaned forward and cut the deck again. They both looked nervously at the card at the top. It was the seven of spades—the illness card. A shudder ran up and down Sasha's spine. She quickly cut again. There was the ace of spades—death. Sasha and her aunt's eyes met apprehensively.

"Nonsense," her aunt said, trying to dismiss the subject. "Forget it and let's have some tea. Go and call your mother." She rose and despite her years moved quickly over to the table in the corner and began to fix the tea. Sasha glanced hesitantly at her aunt and then headed up the stairs.

Her mother's room was dim, lit only by a small kerosene lamp which gave the room a pale cast and a peculiar odor. Her mother lay, face to the wall, with her legs pulled up close to her. She was shivering.

"Mamma!" Sasha cried. "What's the matter?"

"I'm cold . . . very cold . . . please cover me up," Sonya mumbled.

Sasha pulled the covers over her mother. She touched her neck and head. They were burning. She took her mother's temperature. It was dangerously high. Sasha undressed her quickly and covered her with quilts. Suddenly she heard a creaking sound. It was her aunt, a cup of tea in her hand, looking pitifully small in the doorway, her face immeasurably sad.

For three days the women nursed Sofya Andreyevna. She was suffering from pneumonia, as had
her daughter Masha and her husband. At times her
breathing was heavy and she coughed uncontrolla-
bly. But she did not complain and was quiet as she
had been when she underwent her operation years
before.

On the third day she called her daughters into the
room and said, "I want to tell you before I die. I
think of your father always. I live with him all the
time, and torment myself for not having been good
enough for him. But I was faithful to him body and
soul. I was only eighteen when I married him, but I
never loved anyone but him."

Sasha looked into her mother's large, dark eyes.
Tears streamed down her face. This was the woman
who had loved Vanichka better than her, whom she
had always blamed for her father's unhappiness, and
whom she thought she could never, never forgive.
She was dying. And now none of it mattered. Sasha
felt ashamed. Ashamed of the hate and hurt she had
carried within her for so long.

The following day Sofya Andreyevna Behrs
Tolstoy died. A week later Sasha and her sister
Tanya sorted through their mother's clothes. A
flannel dressing gown or a piece of fabric could fetch
flour and sugar. An old jacket might bring a slab of
bacon. In hard times like these no one could afford
the luxury of mourning.

Sasha placed the bundle of clothes in a sleigh and
drove to a prosperous village thirteen miles from
Yasnaya Polyana. When she arrived, she went into a
familiar two-room izba she had often visited in her

youth. Sasha's eyes scanned the main room. It was large and a giant pech, or clay stove, dominated one wall. Above it were sleeping platforms, so typical of peasant huts. The heat from the stove kept them warm, protecting the inhabitants from freezing in their sleep. The walls were bare save for a few icons which hung in a corner. Sasha was surprised to see them. The Soviet government frowned upon religion and in many peasant homes they had been taken down. In the opposite corner, facing the stove, was a large rough-hewn table with benches running along the two adjoining walls to form an "L." The table was laid out with ham and bacon and black bread. A samovar was bubbling on it as well, and the rich, rare, smell of coffee filled the room. Three old grandmothers sat on the far tablebench.

When Sasha drew close, two rose and nodded. Sasha put her bundle on the bench and opened it. Each article was carefully examined by the old woman. Each hole or stain was noted. Then the bargaining began.

"Five pounds of rye for this petticoat . . . not a gram over six and the scarf to boot . . ."

Sasha was used to such haggling from her selling in the open-air market. She argued with them, always firm with her trades. When the women finally reached an impasse, the third peasant turned to Sasha.

"I want to ask you, Alexandra Lvovna. I don't understand why, after being so rich, having such a great estate, you are exchanging old clothes for bread. Where have all your riches gone? If I were you, I'd just order them 'Bring me so many pounds of wheat and rye and buckwheat from the store-house!'"

Sasha smiled sadly. Like so many of the older peasants the woman did not understand the change brought about by the new regime. She was wary of change. "Everything belongs to the government now," Sasha said. "If I order grain, or if I take it myself, they'll put me in prison!"

But the old woman kept on. "What right have they to take what belongs to you? How can you go on living?"

Sasha remained silent. She had wondered that herself. But she had faith that there was a reason for whatever lay ahead. Somehow she would learn to endure.

The woman told the others to be generous to the "count's" daughter, adding, "If the masters did not need food so badly, do you think they would come and offer us all these old clothes of theirs?"

The old woman remembered a time when the master would ride across the fields on his fine horse and stop for a chat and some tea. And he would tip her for her hospitality. Sometimes a whole gold piece. Then she would bow and say, "Thank you, your excellency. I wish you good health, your excellency."

Yes, Sasha remembered such a time. But it was far-off and distant now. What lay ahead she did not know. But there'd be bacon and buckwheat on her aunt's and sister's table tomorrow and enough flour to last through the long winter ahead.

16

Sasha returned to Moscow by train. There was much work to be done if she was ever to convert Yasnaya Polyana into a museum and model school. The new government's strict rules and regulations made executing the smallest plan a major effort. Each change had to be approved by a board; each requisition involved frustrating red tape. It seemed to Sasha that she was traveling endlessly between Yasnaya Polyana and Moscow on lice-ridden freights, forever sandwiched between equally weary and hungry travelers.

In March she returned from one such trip on the verge of exhaustion. All she could think of was a hot bath, a strong cup of tea and her warm bed. Her eyes were swollen and her feet ached terribly from the twenty-hour stand. She walked slowly back to her apartment. Her heavy bag, filled with books and plans, was swung across one shoulder. Sasha sighed as she looked up the stairway toward her rooms. She was ready to drop. At least that bath and bed were close. But at the top of the stairs she saw that her door was sealed and a piece of paper was plastered to it. It was the seal of the Cheka—the new secret police. It forbade her to enter and commanded her to make contact with them immediately. Bewildered, Sasha hurried to the public phone located at the end of the hall. A curt voice told her that officers would be arriving shortly and that she was to wait for them. He would not tell her what she had done or where they were taking her.

Two uniformed men arrived within ten minutes. They gruffly pushed past her and began searching her rooms. When they finished they turned to her for the first time and ordered her to pack whatever she could carry in one bag.

"Why?" she asked, astounded.

"You are under arrest," one of the officers replied matter-of-factly.

"Arrested? What for? You didn't find anything."

"There is an order to arrest you."

"Impossible," Sasha pleaded. "Absolutely impossible. Why, I am the commissar of Yasnaya Polyana. I have had nothing to do with politics. This is a terrible misunderstanding."

"Please get your things," the officer repeated.

Sasha was taken to the infamous Lubyanka prison where many of the government's worst enemies were imprisoned. All sharp objects—scissors, penknife, tweezers—were taken from her.

"Do you remember having meetings in your rooms?" the magistrate asked her later that day.

"No, I don't," Sasha answered firmly, but suddenly she knew what this was about. More than a year before some friends had borrowed her rooms for meetings. She was not told anything about them, nor did she ask. Once or twice she had warmed the samovar and served them tea. But whenever she entered the room all conversation had ceased. Now it became clear that the meetings had been of a political nature. The government assumed she, like the others, was plotting against the new regime. She began to realize the seriousness of her situation.

After the interrogation she was taken to a tiny cell. It was totally empty save for a single chair placed directly in the center of the room. Wearily, Sasha curled up in the chair and wrapped her blanket around her. She tried not to think about the arrest. In fact, she was so tired she could hardly believe what had happened. She was sure that when she woke up she would find this was a terrible dream, brought on by exhaustion. Somewhere in the room she could hear pattering sounds . . . perhaps there were rats. If only it wasn't so dark. She envisioned them crawling onto the chair and creeping over her. Sasha pulled her blanket even closer about her and managed to fall asleep. In the morning when she awoke she felt something soft on her breast and cheek. Shuddering violently, she shook herself. A huge rat thudded to the ground. It had not been a dream.

Two soldiers took her to another cell where a group of women sat at a table ripping cigarette boxes into pieces.

"Is your name Tolstoy?" an elderly woman asked.

A cigarette butt drooped from her lower lip.

"Yes," Sasha replied, wondering how this woman knew who she was.

"We are making playing cards out of these cigarette boxes. Oh, this is your bed," she said pointing to the wooden cot nearest the door.

Sasha looked from the bed to the rest of the room. It was a long and narrow cell, with two small windows, each heavily barred. All the cots were against one wall, opposite the table and chairs.

"I am a doctor," the woman added, "Petrovskaya is my name. A political prisoner."

Another woman, younger and more attractive, started to speak to Sasha in French. Everyone turned toward her to see if she would reply. But Sasha just stood looking at her cellmates.

"Have you got rats?" she finally asked.

"Not many," the old woman, Petrovskaya, answered. "The guard brings us a cat once in a while."

Sasha threw her bag under the cot and sat down.

For two months she lived in this cell, getting to know these women and becoming tired of them as only one locked up in a single room, day after day, can. Each day they cried, they complained, they walked the floors, they went over their arrest.

"Enough smoking, doctor! The cell is full of smoke. There is no air to breathe!" the typist would complain. "Stop pacing back and forth like that. You make me nervous!"

"My soul aches," the doctor would reply. "I have no peace day or night. I got my husband mixed up in this business and he's arrested too. It's my fault. I am responsible."

"You know," the French woman would say, paying no attention to the doctor or the typist, "when you speak to the examining magistrate you must put on a little rouge, you must smile too, gradually he will smile as well."

"Were you smiling when they arrested you?" someone would ask.

After a while, Sasha stopped listening to their words. Each morning she got up, exercised, and waited for her bread and watered-down soup. Each night she rushed through her bath and toilet in the allotted two minutes. She tried not to think about the glorious Moscow spring outside the barred windows or of her sister and friends. But she did find herself thinking about the nature of freedom. Here she was, locked up, for a ridiculous crime—lighting the samovar. Others were jailed for even less. Did they actually do something against the state? Or was it their very existence that was threatening? Was the name of Tolstoy still too powerful and were they trying to weaken it by casting a bad light on his daughter? Or was it simply that they did not know what to make of her? She wondered often what her father would have done in this situation. Was this any worse than living in a place that denied your nature or went against your beliefs? Or worse than being forced to perform acts you did not believe in? Wasn't this similar to the immobility and lack of freedoms the aristocracy had foisted upon the peasants? What was the true nature of freedom, then?

In May Sasha was released pending trial. She packed the single bag they had allowed her and quickly said good-bye. As she left the cell she looked hard at the women she had lived with for two months. Suddenly she grabbed a pencil and wrote in large black letters on the white wall opposite the door: "The holy spirit in everyone of us is free. No bars, no guards, no prison walls can deprive us of our freedom!"

Sasha went back to her apartment. She felt unsteady. She could not settle down to work at Yasnaya or in Moscow. She was afraid to speak to anyone, afraid they were spies—informers. At night she rushed through her washing up as she had in prison. She slept with her blankets wrapped tightly about her. Every day she waited for notification of the trial. At last it came.

On the appointed day Sasha walked to the courthouse. She was wearing a white dress. She entered the court cautiously. The five friends she had lent her rooms to sat on benches in front. Her sister Tanya sat high in the gallery.

Sasha sat toward the back of the room where she could watch the prosecution at work. An armed guard tapped her shoulder and insisted she sit in front with the other defendants. All day the jury heard the accounts of the meetings and backgrounds of the six on trial. At the end of the day they were taken to the Lubyanka and locked in a large, empty room.

In the morning they returned to court. Sasha's dress was crumpled and stained. It felt to her like a dirty rag. She ran her fingers through her matted hair. She could see her sister's pained face gazing down at her. She turned away.

Sasha was the last defendant to speak.

"Citizen Tolstoy," the prosecutor began, "what was your role at the meetings?"

"My role?" Sasha asked. "My role consisted of heating the samovar."

"And serving tea."

"Yes, and serving tea."

"That was the only part you had in this business?"

"Yes," she answered.

An hour later the jury brought in their verdict. The five group members were sentenced to death for treason, although they were released from prison after ten years at hard labor. Alexandra Lvovna Tolstoy was accused of counterrevolutionary activities against the state and sentenced to three years in a prison camp. Many considered her sentence light.

17

Two armed soldiers led Sasha and another woman prisoner out of the Lubyanka. They were being taken to Novospasky Monastery. The day was hot and Sasha's bag weighed heavily on her shoulder. The soldiers were unfriendly and insisted they walk down the middle of the cobblestone street in plain view. Sasha didn't mind the humiliation—the trial and the two months locked up in a tiny cell with five complaining, frantic women had numbed her senses and her pride. But the bag was heavy, the cobblestones were sharp underfoot, and the monastery-turned-prison was clear across Moscow. After several miles her feet were red and swollen.

"Comrades," she asked her guards. "Please let us walk on the sidewalk. Our feet are sore." But the soldiers simply shrugged and said, "Not allowed." Just then the sky darkened and it began to rain. The guards ran for cover and signaled for their prisoners to follow. Sasha realized that this was her chance to get on the soldiers' better side. She reached deep into her bag and pulled out a battered cigarette case which had been given to her during the war.

"Would you like a cigarette?" she asked them, smiling. They nodded and each took one from the case. Then she bent down and pulled her shoes and stockings off. There was a drainpipe nearby and she walked barefoot over to it. Her feet were badly blistered. The rushing water felt good. The soldiers looked down and saw that her feet were raw.

"Citizens," one of them said. "You can walk on the sidewalk. It is not allowed, but you have been kind and your feet look as if they have been scalded."

The rest of the way to the monastery was more pleasant, the soldiers and their prisoners walking side by side. They began to converse and eventually they asked Sasha the length of her sentence.

"Three years!" Sasha answered in anguish.

"Bad luck. Your youth will be wasted."

Sasha grimaced. Her face might be youthful, but she was thirty-six. She did not have much youth left to waste.

Finally the monastery came into view. Sasha relaxed upon seeing its low white walls and giant shade trees. It reminded her of the serene ancient monasteries her mother had taken her to as a child. Just then, an awful scream followed by a chain of curses shattered the serenity. Two women ran onto the lawn, pushing and scratching each other. They were trying desperately to grab each other's hair. A guard ran over and pulled them into the monastery. Sasha entered the building trembling.

After an interrogation Sasha was handed over to a

woman who was obviously a prisoner herself. She wore a plain cotton blouse and a rough homemade skirt and her feet were bare save for a pair of ragged felt slippers. She led Sasha down a series of long white corridors. When they were a good distance from the interrogation office, the woman turned to Sasha and grabbed her hand warmly.

"Are you the daughter of Lev Nikolayevich?" she whispered. There was excitement in her voice.

Sasha did not answer. She was still thinking about the two women outside.

"Dear Alexandra Lvovna, don't be distressed. We can live anywhere. It all depends on our inner peace. And this place is not so dreadful as it seems at first. Believe me, you can be happy anywhere."

The woman's name was Olga. The daughter of a governor, she was jailed for no other crime than being just that. A woman with dark bobbed hair turned onto their corridor and stood facing them. She glanced questioningly at the governor's daughter.

"Anna Federovna," Olga said. "Have we a spare cot in our room? This is Alexandra Lvovna, the daughter of Tolstoy!" The woman with the bobbed hair waved for them to follow her. At the end of the corridor she turned into a low-ceilinged room with an unpainted floor, small windows and a blue-tiled stove. It had obviously been a monk's cell before the revolution. Sasha began to relax. Although it was stark, the room was clean, and the tiled stove gave it warmth.

An old woman in a black cotton dress and a white shawl rose from her bed and bowed slowly as they entered.

"Aunt Liza," Anna Federovna said, "did you ever hear of Lev Tolstoy, the writer? This is his daughter."

The old woman looked at Sasha as if remembering. "Of course, of course," she said at last. "A strange place to meet her, though. Ah, but God knows what He is doing."

A tall striking woman entered the cell. She had silky gray hair and wore an old-fashioned pinch-waisted dress. Sasha instantly recognized her. She was a well-known baroness and society woman. *So these are the women I am to spend the next three years of my life with,* Sasha thought. Given the circumstances, she was pleased. They seemed sincere and bright and not at all like those women she had seen on the lawn . . . nor like the doctor and the typist!

Sasha lived in a cell with political prisoners, all of whom were educated to some degree. But the monastery was filled with women who could not write or read. Many were criminals who had lived on their own since childhood. They cursed like men and knew nothing at all of bodily care.

Sasha decided that as long as she was to be in prison, she must continue her work. These women needed to learn. Perhaps with some basic education they could find honest work when free. Perhaps she could even start a physical fitness program to help them build both their bodies and their spirits. The inactivity of prison life seemed to break people's spirits more than anything else. Sasha went to the warden and pleaded for his approval. He gave it and even allowed Sasha to make several trips into the city for books. Soon Sasha was busy every afternoon with her lessons. And the response surprised her. It seemed there were many inmates who had never been given the opportunity to learn, but hungered for knowledge.

Every morning after Sasha awoke, she began her physical fitness program, along with her fellow cell-mates and some of her students. After breakfast she began classes in a large empty laundry room. In the evenings she wrote in her journal, describing her daily lessons and future classes. Sometimes small resolutions mingled with her notes: "I must rise earlier," "I must pray harder," "I must be more patient." On weekends she often met with the other prisoners to discuss conditions and how they could be improved. Although they would voice their discontent, few dared hope for change. It was rumored that at least half of the prisoners' daily rations were stolen by the warden. But everyone was afraid to complain. They were afraid of his punishment, which could be harsh.

So they made do with the daily rations they got—sugar, butter, bread. Each morning Anna Federovna spread newspapers onto the table and cut the butter, which was usually marked with dirty fingerprints, into sections. Then she passed out the sugar and soup, when there was any. It was usually made of frozen potato peels. Grit always floated on its surface. One had to wait for it to settle on the bottom before eating. Once in a while they were given salted dry fish. But it was always too dry to eat. Sasha beat it furiously against the gravestones outside until it softened and the roe fell out. Sometimes it took a full fifteen minutes.

Sasha and Anna were the only two members of the

cell to receive packages from home. Once a month Tanya visited. She always carried a package with her, which contained whatever bits of food she could scrape up. It pained Sasha to see the look of horror on her sister's face whenever she visited or the way she lifted her skirts as she walked across the lawn. She knew that the coarse language of the inmates and the very nature of the place disturbed her. And so she was always glad when the visit was over and her sister could escape. But Sasha looked forward to those visits more than her sister knew.

Prison common law dictated that everything received from the outside be shared with cellmates. Accordingly, after each of Tanya's visits, Sasha passed out whatever the package contained. The Red Cross also sent packages each month containing sugar, sunflower oil, and cigarettes. The cellmates always tried to save the contents of whichever package came first until the other arrived. Then they'd have a party. They'd light the fire, soak the bread in oil and fry it, and drink tea heavily sweetened with sugar or jam. The five women would sit in front of the blue-tiled stove and tell stories of their days of freedom. Between the warmth and the camaraderie they sometimes even forgot where they were.

One day a young woman in blue trousers and shirt walked into their cell.

"I am the representative of the Workers' and Peasants' Inspection and also a member of the Women's Department of the Communist party," she began. "Our government is anxious that citizens— workers and peasants—who did wrong under the tsarist regime have a chance to improve. That is why the government is trying to organize educational institutions to spread the idea of our Communist party among the prisoners . . . so that they can be educated in the true spirit of socialism. As soon as you get free, every one of you must join the ranks of the proletariat which is fighting for freedom and the happiness of the working class! Who is doing educational work in the camp?"

Everyone remained silent.

"Who is working with the illiterates?"

"I am."

The woman turned toward Sasha. "And how are you helping Communist propaganda?"

"I am not helping it."

"Why not?"

"Because I do not approve of it."

The young inspector looked at Sasha curiously, but she did not pursue the subject. "Now comrades," she continued, "how is life here? How are you fed? Are you given clothes? Do you get wood for your stove?"

Again no one spoke.

"Comrades," the inspector went on, "are there any questions about the food? How does the warden treat you?"

Sasha looked at the woman before her. "What's the use of asking us all those questions?" she said. "Don't you understand that if we are silent it is not because we don't have anything to complain of. Every one of us knows that if we tell you the truth we will be punished as soon as you leave camp . . . thrown in the cellar or worked to the bone."

But the inspector would not relent. She insisted that nothing would happen to them if they spoke up.

The governor's daughter and Anna Federovna glanced at Sasha.

Sasha sighed. If she was going to get into trouble, at least it would be for standing up for their rights.

"Let me ask you a question," Sasha said. "How can we say anything when we do not know what is due us? We only know that they are feeding us frozen potato skins, that we haven't enough bread, that we are given dirty rags to wear that are good for nothing."

The inspector was taken aback. She assured them that she knew nothing of these conditions and promised to do something about the situation before she left. Within a month the warden was dismissed. But conditions did not change. In the warden's place came others, equally greedy, equally dishonest. The inspector continued to visit the camp and tried to improve the situation as best she could. She often spoke to Sasha about her views.

"Why should you stay in prison?" she would ask. "You could work for us, for the working people."

"What do you think I have been trying to do, both at Yasnaya Polyana and here with the illiterates?" Sasha retorted.

"You are a good teacher and are dedicated. We need people like you," the inspector went on. "You are wasted here. I will try to get you out." True to her word, she arranged an interview for Sasha with the release board.

Meanwhile the peasants of Yasnaya Polyana and two neighboring villages also felt Sasha could do more good out of prison than within. Five peasants came to Moscow to speak with the president of the

111

release board in person. On hearing of the peasants' presence in Moscow, Sasha decided that she had to see them.

She wanted to tell them that whatever happened, she appreciated their efforts. She begged the warden to allow her to visit them in the apartment where they were staying. But he feared her face would be recognized and that he would lose his job. Sasha left his office depressed. How was she going to manage this? Then an idea came to her. Excited, she scurried off down the long corridor.

Half an hour later a stocky peasant woman entered the warden's office. She was dressed in skirt, blouse, and scarf. She had dark eyebrows and painted cheeks and lips.

"What do you want?" the warden asked the woman sharply.

"Of your kindness, father . . ." she said in a squeaky voice. Then she added, "Don't you recognize me?"

The warden looked hard at the peasant woman. Suddenly he realized that he had been duped. "It's you, Comrade Tolstoy!" he exclaimed. "Well! Well! I never would have recognized you!"

She was allowed to go on condition that she return by tea time that evening. It was already turning dark when she set out. She had to walk by lonely river quays to get to the peasants' apartment. Twice soldiers, mistaking her for a lost peasant girl, tried to engage her in conversation, but each time she managed to slip away.

When she arrived she created a sensation. "What

does this masquerade mean? Have you escaped?" the peasants exclaimed in alarm.

Sasha quickly explained the need for the dress and makeup and soon they were deep in conversation, drinking tea and eating the homemade bread they had brought. The peasants told her how her plans for a museum and school had come to nothing in her absence and that even the farmland had not been worked. Her aunt and sister were struggling to make ends meet.

When it was time to go, Sasha once again wrapped her shawl about her and smudged rouge on her cheeks. One of the peasants took the remaining bread and wrapped it in newspaper.

"Take this with you, Alexandra Lvovna. We made it especially for you. Prison food cannot be very good."

Sasha smiled, not knowing what to say. She rested her hand on his shoulder for a brief moment and looked into his eyes. Then she left.

Several months later she was set free.

18

SOON AFTER SASHA WAS RELEASED FROM PRISON she went to Kalinin, the Soviet president under Lenin. After the peasants' visit she realized that her plans for Yasnaya Polyana had not been carried out. If she wanted to turn Yasnaya Polyana into a museum or a school or a cultural haven it was going to be up to her to do it. The more she thought about it the more she realized that Yasnaya Polyana could become an entire Tolstoyan community, including a museum, a library, a hospital, numerous schools offering various programs, and a working farm to help finance the other ventures. Armed with this new concept, she appealed to Kalinin. She relied on the hope that he, like so many, associated her father with revolutionary work since he had stood up against the Tsar, the church, and his fellow nobility so many times. He did, and within three months she was hard at work turning her plans into a reality.

Sasha immediately hired the few remaining

Tolstoyans to help with the museum, a bookkeeper to keep records of all transactions, and an overseer to help run the farm. The work was mammoth and it soon became clear that everyone, even the well-manicured bookkeeper, had to lend a hand. It was not unusual to find the entire staff out in the fields.

"Go away! Go lie down on the stove!" the younger assistants would shout on seeing old Ilya Vasilievich, the valet, pushing a wheelbarrow. "The cart is too heavy for you," someone would scold. But everyone wanted to work, and throughout the summer they dug, plowed, and raked. They planted herbs and vegetables, potatoes and beets, remaining in the fields long after the villagers finished their eight-hour days. Once in a while the peasants would visit Sasha in the fields, and when they told her that her crops were better than their own and that she truly was her father's daughter, she beamed with delight. There was no greater compliment.

When autumn came and the harvest was in, Sasha and her helpers turned their attention to opening the schools. The old cow barn, complete with an ancient Swiss bull, soon became an "industrial" school. The instructor, a jolly fair-haired carpenter, put his eager students to work laying floors, painting walls, making workbenches. A simple hut in the village was transformed into a primary school. Within months it was filled to capacity. When a Jewish-American organization donated ten thousand rubles to the community, yet another school was opened. Youngsters flocked to the schools. As soon as one opened, it filled with students. When ten orphans mysteriously appeared on the estate, Sasha opened an orphanage. When the

115

American Relief Association presented her with medical supplies and instruments, she started a dispensary.

The schools and orphanage grew and grew. Children from distant villages came on foot and begged admittance. Sasha could not bear to turn them away. The houses in the village were filled with industrial-school students. Often they worked late into the night making tables and chairs to take to their families on weekends. Orphaned children were constantly being sent to Sasha. "Send him to Alexandra Lvovna. She will take care of him and educate and feed him," the villagers would say on hearing of yet another homeless child. And sure enough, she always did.

But the care of so many children and the maintenance of so many schools took funds. And the profits from the harvest quickly ran out. Sasha spent endless afternoons in the reception rooms of commissars explaining her situation, begging for government money. Sometimes she found a sympathetic ear and sometimes she did not. The dedicated teachers remained on little, if any, salary while the less dedicated teachers deserted. Sasha began raising bees and selling honey in Tula to supplement their income. It was a hard life and needed all the strength she had, but she did not give up and felt that she was truly carrying on her father's work.

When an agent from the trade union came to Yasnaya Polyana collecting money for the military Sasha turned him away. "Tolstoy was a pacifist. We do our work in his name and cannot support military organizations." When visitors came to the museum

116

she told them of her father's beliefs and work. But such independence in a newly formed Communist country was unique and could not last.

In 1923 Lenin died and his associate, Stalin, took over. Stalin was a strict Communist and looked suspiciously on any organization that did not further his cause. It was only a matter of time before his agents became aware of the little Tolstoyan community prospering in their midst.

19

"SECLUDING THEMSELVES ON THE ESTATE," THE article in the national newspaper, *Pravda*, read, "a former countess and other members of the bourgeoisie are living at Yasnaya Polyana and holding to their old practices. They have orgies, they make museum janitors serve them and keep the samovars lighted all night long . . . as a reward for a night's work, they throw them crumbs from the table!"

Sasha read the article in disbelief. She hardly knew what to make of it . . . orgies! crumbs! Who would say such things about her and her little community? Government officials descended on Yasnaya Polyana before she had time to find out. They searched her office, they interrogated the teachers, they spoke secretly with her students. In the village, Communists seized the opportunity to lecture the peasants about "the bourgeois exploiters who have found refuge with that rascal Alexandra Tolstoy." Such talk did not impress the old peasants who knew of the good she had achieved, but the younger ones listened. Workers refused to take orders. At night young gangs carved Communist messages on the estate's benches and littered the lawns with paper and sunflower seeds. The entire household was agitated over the drastic change that had taken place . . . even Sasha's aunt Tanya, who was often bedridden these days, spoke of punishing the young activists. Sasha appealed to Kalinin once again and he promised there would be a complete, impartial investigation of the paper's accusations.

Meanwhile her teachers grew frightened that the Bolsheviks would imprison them for their connection with Alexandra Tolstoy. "Something has got to be done," they insisted. "We can't live under the constant threat of being driven out or put in prison." "We can't do anything," Sasha replied over and over. "We must wait patiently for the committee of inquiry." "It will never come and in the meantime they will ruin all our work," the teachers complained.

But Kalinin's committee did come.

"When did you have a banquet with wine?" the inspector asked.

"On the twenty-third of April. It was my name day," Sasha answered, wondering what this had to do with the accusations.

"How many people were there?"

"About forty."

"How much wine did you have?"

"Two bottles of port."

The members of the committee looked at each other.

"Is Citizen Tolstoy telling the truth?" they asked

119

the janitor, Tolkach, who it seemed had accused Sasha of "bourgeois activities."

"Well, I guess she is," he answered.

"Didn't Tolkach light the samovar for you at two in the morning?" the inspector asked Sasha.

"Yes, he did. But I will tell you how that happened and Tolkach will correct me if I'm mistaken. Tolkach was on night duty. I invited him to join the party and have tea with us. He seemed pleased, joined us, sang songs with us. At two o'clock in the morning, my assistant—seeing that the samovar was empty—started for the kitchen to refill it for us. But Tolkach was very nice about it. He got up, took the samovar and heated it himself and he was the first to get a cup of hot tea."

"Is that right, Comrade Tolkach?"

"Yes."

"Comrade Tolkach told me about the incident from a somewhat different point of view," the inspector said, looking at the janitor angrily.

Sasha continued her story. "When the party was over, about three, I thought of Tolkach's wife and children, wrapped up some apple pie and candy and handed them to him. I hadn't the slightest intention of offending him and he did not seem to take it that way."

When the interview ended and it was obvious that Alexandra Lvovna had been wronged, the committee asked Sasha what she wanted them to do.

"I want a retraction of the newspaper article," she answered immediately.

They agreed and it appeared, but it was not the end of the situation. The government's attention was now firmly on Yasnaya Polyana and there was nothing Sasha could do to direct it elsewhere. As Stalin's power grew each day, Sasha's position weakened. His means of keeping the people in line and making sure the Bolshevik Revolution was complete was through force. Peasants who seemed to be doing too well were reprimanded, even persecuted. When food production dropped, Stalin pressured the peasants to join farm collectives. He made sure that a proper balance of education and Communist propaganda was taught in the schools. With Stalin at the government's head now, it was foolhardy for Sasha to think things could be as free as they were under Lenin.

She watched as one student group, the Komsomol, grew stronger and stronger in her schools. The Komsomol was a branch of the newly formed Young Communist League. Members, who had to be between fifteen and twenty-eight years of age, were expected to spread Communist teachings, gain support for and increase membership in the Communist party. Pressure to join was intense. Membership became a prerequisite to college. Many of Sasha's best students, not wanting to join the political group, dropped out. The Komsomol exerted peer pressure to reject past traditions and beliefs. But there were still some students who found it difficult to give up the traditions so deeply a part of Russian culture. Many of the parents still prayed to icons and secretly celebrated Easter. Yet many, born during the Revolution, had never been taught religion, many had never seen a Bible.

Once while passing a classroom, Sasha heard loud

voices coming from within. Curious, she walked in.

"Oh, I'm glad you've come" the teacher said. She looked anxious and flushed. "Please tell us what you think of God."

"God?" Sasha asked in disbelief.

"Yes! Yes!" one of the children shouted. "We want to know whether God exists or not."

"Of course He does, children," Sasha answered, not looking at the teacher, who, she knew, expected a different response.

"No! It's only the bourgeoisie who believe in God. And the priests darken the poor people's minds and then rob them," a Komsomol youth shouted back. "Marx said that religion is the opiate of the people. It numbs them into inactivity. We must fight it and work for the country!"

"My parents believe in God. They haven't thrown their icons away," someone added.

"Pieces of wood," another child said angrily.

"Who created the world if not God?" a peasant girl asked quietly.

They implored Sasha to stay and answer their questions. What had her father believed? Were all the priests truly greedy? What about reincarnation? She answered their questions frankly. She could not lie to them. She could not allow herself to become a spokeswoman for a government that held beliefs she could never accept. Everywhere Sasha looked she saw people suppressing their true feelings and going with the general opinion. It was difficult to stand firm against an entire system. In her schools she now had little support, at home she had no one to talk to—her Aunt Tanya had died, her sister, whose husband had

122

died as well, had a brood of children to care for and problems of her own, her brothers were scattered in Russia and abroad, most of her father's old allies were dead. The Tolstoyans had long ago deserted her in search of more popular causes. People were constantly seeking her out, knowing that she did not fear the Soviets or their threats. Every time she went to Moscow the phone rang persistently. It was always the same—someone's husband was arrested, someone's books were being banned . . . Could she help? Could she appeal? Sasha went to the officials, she tried to help, she tried to argue. It was a hard road to take by oneself. As a child Sasha had had difficulty speaking out, it had been a long time before she had been able to speak her mind, but since then she had always stood up to those she disagreed with and fought for those things she held dear. And so she spoke out, always at great personal risk. Each time she argued, each time she tried to fight, her name was written down on yet another suspicious-persons list.

In 1929 she received an order from the commissar of education informing her that the schools were to remain open on Easter Sunday. Sasha called a meeting of teachers. She knew that many of them, like the villagers, closed their doors on that holy day and painted eggs with their children and ate two Easter treats called kuetchi and pashki. But the teachers voted to uphold the order. They were afraid.

"Comrades," Sasha said at the meeting, "until now you have had faith in me and believed that I could lead the schools in a spirit of independence and freedom. You followed me and helped me. Now I feel that you no longer trust me and I cannot work with you anymore." Sasha looked sadly at her fellow teachers. She started to speak again, but could not find the words and had to leave the room. The schools, the museum, the hospital, had become too big for her to control. She knew the end had come. She would not be a puppet of her own creation.

She went out onto Yasnaya Polyana hill. From there she looked down over the fields. The ice was melting into the Voronka River and the meadows were filled with water. Everything looked peaceful, but she knew in her heart that something had changed and it would never be the same again. For the first time she regretted that all this had been created in her father's name.

20

"I CAN NO LONGER WORK AS DIRECTOR OF THE Yasnaya Polyana schools. I simply can't go on." Sasha stood awkwardly in front of the commissar of education. He was a slight man, and the fact that he sat while she stood made her even more aware than usual of her large frame. She felt that she towered above him.

"Why can't you go on?" the small man asked.

"I do not agree with the government's policies."

"For example?"

"I am against mass propaganda in schools and the peasants being forced to join farm collectives."

"We are not forcing them."

Sasha grew flushed. This kind of argument led nowhere. "You are creating such conditions that those who do not want to join collectives are obliged to. Not long ago in a village near Yasnaya Polyana a peasant left a collective and the Communist board refused to give him back his property. He lost everything. He was desperate. Eventually he hanged himself."

The Commissar shook his head and leaned forward in his chair. "I have just come from the country. I visited several collectives. The peasants are satisfied. They are using tractors, they have bought purebred cattle."

"Where were you? Who told you this?" Sasha asked, her voice giving away her annoyance.

"Various places. The peasants told me how happy they were, and of course, no one knew who I was." The Commissar leaned back in his chair, pleased with himself.

Sasha did not reply. He was convinced that he had traveled incognito, but she knew that a peasant could spot a commissar from far away. Usually by the time one arrived in a village, the entire area knew who he was, where he came from, and what he wanted. But there was no point in arguing.

"Please let me resign! I cannot continue working."

"No," he said firmly. "We can't dismiss you . . . we need good teachers."

He looked down at his desk and began reading some papers. Sasha realized the interview was over and left. But she did not give up. She had to find a way. She could not go on working at Yasnaya Polyana. She could not stand by and watch her schools be turned into Bolshevik factories. She had based them on her father's principles. She could not bear to see each principle dismissed, each replaced with militarism, atheism, communism . . .

If they would not accept her resignation and let her remain in the country, the only feasible solution was to leave. But how? They would never allow her to go. They would be too afraid of her speaking out against them. Unless she was leaving to aid the regime.

"Let me go to Japan for three months to study the schools . . . perhaps to America as well. Then I can come back and work with new energy. I am tired," Sasha pleaded with the authorities. She reasoned that they were more likely to let her go to Japan than to Europe, where there were many anti-Bolsheviks and Russian refugees. In Japan there were few Russians and many of the Japanese looked favorably on the new regime.

"You will certainly not come back," one official told her. "If I were in the place of the Central Committee, I would not let you go."

But Sasha argued well: "Aren't the institutions to which I have given so much of my energy sufficient guarantee to you?"

For eight months she repeatedly requested a passport and permission to travel to Japan. She corresponded with Japanese universities about the possibility of a lecture tour on Tolstoy. Eventually she received an invitation. Armed with it she went to the Central Committee.

"If you will not let me go," she threatened, "I shall have to reply that I cannot accept because the government authorities are afraid to let me go abroad!"

Within weeks, Sasha received a small red passport. The photograph inside showed a forty-six-year-old woman with a broad face and fair hair pulled back into a bun at the nape of her neck. Small wrinkles were beginning to appear around her eyes and mouth. She wore thick glasses. The years in prison and the constant pressures at Yasnaya Polyana had indeed robbed her of her youth. But they had given her a clear picture of what she must now dedicate herself to: the task of helping people free themselves from persecution. She had seen firsthand how people could be imprisoned for nothing more than being the daughter of a governor. She had seen how people could deny their own convictions out of fear. And she had seen how, despite political change and propaganda, children could yearn for answers to age-old questions. Somewhere there existed a place where one could be free to act and believe as one saw fit. In that place she would dedicate herself to helping those who could not help themselves.

Sasha quickly began work on her lecture outline. Everything had to be approved by the government. When she finished she was required to take them and her books, notes, addresses, and photographs to the nearest Soviet. They were packed and sealed so that unapproved items could not be added.

There were those who suspected Sasha would not return, but few spoke of it. She tried to act as if she were going on a three-month holiday, but in her heart she knew it might be years before she saw Yasnaya Polyana again.

"But you will come back?" Ilya Vasilievich said softly, his white-gloved hand in Sasha's.

"Of course I will, Ilya. Take care of yourself and my family while I'm away. Don't think of dying!"

The old man looked at Sasha sadly. He had known her since she was born, and had worked for the master long before that. Tears rolled down his weathered face. "Please come back as quickly as possible," he said, his voice shaking.

Suddenly it was time to leave. The old family carriage arrived, drawn by two of Sasha's favorite stallions, now old themselves. Sasha lifted her bags into the carriage and jumped in without looking back. She told the driver to ride across the orchard to the main road. A quick break, away from the main house and its memories, was best. Soon it and the fields were in the distance . . . she could no longer see the land she had always loved.

Sasha was leaving her childhood, her mother, her father, Vanichka, Masha, the peasants . . . everything she had ever known or been influenced by. What lay ahead she did not know. But of one thing she was certain. She would return only when the Bolsheviks were no longer in power and her people were free. Then and only then could she go home and take up her work. She was sure this change would come and that someday she would set foot on Russian soil again.

EPILOGUE

ALEXANDRA LVOVNA TOLSTOY LEFT RUSSIA IN
1929. She remained in Japan two years, where she
lectured on Russia and her famous father. In 1931
she arrived in the United States, a penniless refugee,
having defied the Soviet authorities' command to
return home. For eight years she struggled to survive
the depression, working as an egg farmer and sometime lecturer.

In April 1939 Sasha started the Tolstoy Foundation. It was dedicated to assisting victims of oppression and resettling them in the free world. Sasha
restricted her efforts to Soviet refugees at first,
planning to expand as the foundation grew. And
grow it did. Given a seventy-eight-acre farm by a
sympathetic New York farmer, Sasha set to work
converting barns and outbuildings. By the time
World War II broke out she was equipped to handle
the huge task of processing and caring for the
homeless. Sixty-five hundred people came to her
Reed Farm Resettlement Center. Another thirty
thousand were sponsored by the foundation and
relocated across America under a special legislation
of Congress.

After the war the charter was changed so that
people of all nations could be assisted. Since that
time, thirty-five hundred people a year have been

resettled. Among those assisted have been Czechs, Tibetans, Jews, Himalayans, Armenians, South Americans, Vietnamese and Cambodian Boat People. It is now believed that Alexandra Lvovna Tolstoy and her foundation have relocated one hundred thousand refugees.

On September 26, 1979, Sasha died. She was ninety-five years old and the last of Lev Tolstoy's numerous children. She had not set foot on Russian soil in fifty years.

BIBLIOGRAPHY

Adams, Arthur, E. *Imperial Russia After 1961*. Boston: D.C. Heath, 1965.

Cherniavsky, Michael, ed. *The Structure of Russian History*. New York: Random House, 1970.

Edwards, Anne. *Sonya*. New York: Simon and Schuster, 1981.

Field, Daniel. *Rebels in the Name of the Tsar*. Boston: Houghton Mifflin, 1976.

Massie, Robert. *Nicholas and Alexandra*. New York: Atheneum, 1968.

Miller, Wright. *Russians as People*. New York: Dutton, 1960.

————. *Who Are the Russians?* New York: Taplinger Pub. Co., 1973.

Newman, E.M. *Seeing Russia*. New York: Funk & Wagnalls, 1928.

Robinson, Geroid Tanquary. *Rural Russia Under the Old Regime*. University of California Press, 1960.

Riasanovsky, Nicholas. *A History of Russia*. Oxford University Press, 1969.

Simmons, Ernest J. *Leo Tolstoy*. Boston: Little, Brown, 1946.

Sukhotin, Tatyana (Tolstoy). *The Tolstoy Home*—Diaries. London: Haverill, 1950.

————. *Tolstoy Remembered*. New York: McGraw-Hill, 1977.

Tolstoy, Alexandra Lvovna (Sasha). *A Life of My Father*. New York: Harper, 1953.

————. *I Worked for the Soviet*. New Haven: Yale University Press, 1934.

———. *Out of the Past.* New York: Columbia University Press, 1981.

———. *The Tragedy of Tolstoy.* New Haven: Yale University Press, 1933.

Tolstoy, Ilya Lvovich. *Tolstoy, My Father.* Chicago: Regnery, 1971.

Tolstoy, Lev Lvovich. *The Truth About My Father.* London: J. Murray, 1924.

Tolstoy, Lev Nikolayevich. *Recollections and Essays.* London: Oxford University Press, 1928–37.

Tolstoy, Sergei Lvovich. *Tolstoy Remembered by His Son.* New York: Atheneum, 1961.

Tolstoy, Sofya Andreyevna. *The Autobiography of Countess Sophie Tolstoi.* Richmond, England: Woolf, 1922.

Troyat, Henri. *Tolstoy.* New York: Doubleday, 1967.

Walsh, Warren B., ed. *Readings in Russian History.* Syracuse: Syracuse University Press, 1963.

Wilson, Edmund. *A Window on Russia.* New York: Farrar, Straus & Giroux, 1972.

ADDITIONAL READING: Books by Leo Tolstoy: *Anna Karenina; Childhood; Boyhood; Youth; The Death of Ivan Ilych; The Devil; Hadji Murád; The Kreutzer Sonata; Resurrection; War and Peace.*

INDEX

135

Serfs, emancipation of, 26–27
Soviet
    defined, 52
    See also Bolsheviks
Stalin, Joseph, 117, 121
Sukhotin (Tatyana Tolstoy's
        husband; brother-in-
        law), 34, 123
Sukhotin, Misha (step-
        nephew), 40–42
Sukhotin, Tatyana (Tanya)
        Lvovna, *see* Tolstoy,
        Tatyana (Tanya)
        Lvovna

Tolkach (janitor), 120
Tolstoy, Alexandra (Sasha)
        Lvovna, 31, 77–78,
        81–82
    arrest and imprisonment of,
        98–100, 104–13
    confrontation during,
        109–11
    trial and sentence, 102–3
    working for release of,
        111–13
    childhood of, 3–9, 14–15
    in Moscow, 10–12
    strained family relations
        and, 17–18
    Tolstoyan way of life and,
        7–8
    death of, 13
    dispensary work of, 47–48,
        54
    educational work of, 54, 57
    in prison, 107–8
    See also Tolstoyan com-
        munity
    as exile
    leaves for Japan, 127–30
    settles in U.S., 130
    February revolution and, 80
    her father and, *see* Tolstoy,
        Count Lev (Leo)

Nikolayevich
    her mother and, *see* Tolstoy,
        Sofya (Sonya) An-
        dreyevna
    illness of, 46–47
    Ivan and
    comparison between, 19
    his death and, 20–22, 57
    Khodynka Meadow tragedy
        and, 31, 32
    Masha and
    Masha's death and, 57
    relationship between,
        11–12, 15
    1905 revolution and, 53
    in post-revolutionary period
        (1917)
    Bolsheviks seize property
        of, 84–86
    trading clothes for food,
        90–91, 95–96
    Russo-Japanese War and,
        50
    spiritual rebirth of, 34–38
    Tanya and
    relationship between,
        11–12, 15
    at Sasha's trial, 102
    visits Sasha in jail, 109
    Tolstoyan community and,
        see Tolstoyan com-
        munity
    Tolstoyan museum and, 91,
        97–98, 102
    at Tsar's coronation, 23–25,
        28–30
    in World War II, 69–76, 87
Tolstoy, Andrei Lvovich
        (brother), 9–11, 22, 50,
        63
Tolstoy, Count Lev (Leo)
    Nikolayevich (father), viii–x,
        10, 39, 106, 107
    death of, 63–64, 67, 91
    effects of 1905 revolution
        on followers of, 58

136

137